Leading With Courage

Nine Critical Behaviors of Effective Leaders and Managers

2nd Edition – Expanded and Updated

Lee H. Eisenstaedt, MBA

Leading
With Courage
Academy

First Edition Design Publishing
Sarasota, Florida USA

Leading With Courage: Nine Critical Behaviors of Effective Leaders and Managers
Copyright ©2019 Lee H. Eisenstaedt

ISBN 978-1506-908-30-4 AMZ PBK
ISBN 978-1506-908-29-8 TRADE PBK
ISBN 978-1506-908-31-1 EBK

LCCN 2019906830

June 2019

Published and Distributed by
First Edition Design Publishing, Inc.
P.O. Box 17646, Sarasota, FL 34276-3217
www.firsteditiondesignpublishing.com

NOTICE TO READERS

Leading With Courage® is a registered Trademark

Leading With Courage: Nine Critical Behaviors of Effective Leaders and Managers is distributed with the understanding that the author and publisher are not rendering professional advice within the publication. If expert assistance is required, the services of a competent professional should be sought.

Special discounts on bulk quantities of this book are available to professional associations, corporations, and other organizations. For details, contact:

Hello@LWCAcademy.com or call (312) 827-2643.

Credits:
Creative Coach: Sarah Victory
Editor: Dan Gershenson
Marketing Advisor: Dan Gershenson

Visit our website at
www.LWCAcademy.com

Testimonials for *Leading With Courage*

*"**Leading With Courage** offers pragmatic, easy to understand advice on making a difference as a leader. Unlike the books that deal with a leader's character and other soft skills, Lee has chosen to focus on behaviors and practical approaches that accelerate the alignment of an organization or team around a few initiatives that will make a difference. Any leader or manager will benefit from the ideas in this easy-to-read book."*

Christine Robins
President & CEO, Char-Broil, LLC

*"**Leading With Courage** does an outstanding job at reminding us of the key lessons many of us learned on our career journeys. They are insightful yet practical. The ideas in the book can also be applied to any type of organization – large and small, for profit and non-profit, publicly held and privately owned, etc. Overall, Lee's goal is to accelerate personal development for current and aspiring leaders and managers to help them make a bigger impact, sooner than expected."*

Patrick O'Brien
Vice Chairman, Paris Presents, Inc.
Chairman & Co-Founder, Patina Solutions

*"The insights and experience in **Leading With Courage** are easy to grasp and implement by CEOs and anyone else charged with leading others. More importantly, the book synthesizes the practical advice of 40 successful CEOs on how to be more effective at executing strategic and operating plans. And who among us wouldn't like to be just a bit better at implementing our plans?"*

Todd Brook
CEO, Envisionit Chicago, LLC

Acknowledgements

This book is the result of the contributions of so many people.

Dan Gershenson, founder of Caliber Brand Strategy + Content Marketing, who was invaluable as an editor and sounding board.

Sarah Victory, with The Victory Company, who served as a mentor and coach for the first edition of this book.

Each of the CEOs, Presidents, Managing Partners and CMOs who shared with me their stories and perspectives. Without them, this book wouldn't have been possible. Period.

Vikas Bhatia, former CEO of Kalki Consulting, a cybersecurity consulting firm and currently Founder & CEO of JustProtect, Inc.

John Borling, retired Major General of the United States Air Force whose military career spanned 37 years, including Head of Operations for Strategic Air Command (SAC), author and Founder of SOS America among so many other notable leadership positions.

Todd Brook, CEO of Envisionit, a digital marketing agency, who, like many of the people interviewed for this book, has so many terrific insights and perspectives that he should be writing a book.

Vinny Caraballo, CEO at Global Targeting, Inc. and serving on the faculty of Capella University.

Najib Fayad, former CEO of Nelsons in the UK, who also held leadership positions in the USA, France, South America, South East Asia, Saudi Arabia/Gulf and Middle East with SC Johnson & Son and Proctor & Gamble.

Dan Formeller, Chairman of Tressler, LLP, an eight-office law firm that is headquartered in Chicago.

Gay Gaddis, Founder & CEO of T3, the largest woman-owned advertising agency in the U.S.

Maribel Gerstner, former President and Chief Operating Officer of Allstate Financial Services and Allstate Financial Advisors

Aaron Gillum, Managing Director at Caerus Investment Partners, a venture capital firm in Chicago.

Brian Grady, CEO of Gorilla Group, a provider of e-commerce solutions with headquarters in Chicago and five other offices in the US, Canada and Europe.

Tom Kinder, Office Managing Partner of the Chicago office of Plante & Moran, PLLC.

Mary Richards Lawrence, President of Richards Graphic Communications, a family-owned business.

Pam Lenehan, author, director of three publicly traded companies and former managing director on Wall Street.

Michelle Mason, President & CEO of the Association Forum

David Nissen, Managing Partner of Mueller & Co.

Mary O'Brien, former CEO at Fox Valley Orthopedic Institute

Patrick O'Brien, Vice Chairman of Paris Presents, Inc., a branded cosmetics appliance company, and Chairman and Co-Founder of Patina Solutions.

Adriano Pedrelli, President and CEO at WasteDry, LLC, former President and CEO of Blue Stream Group, and former member of the Board of Directors of Wintrust Financial Corporation.

Jude Rake, Founder and CEO of JDR Growth Partners and two-time CEO.

Brad Rex, former President and CEO at Foundation Partners Group, a roll-up of nearly 90 funeral homes and former Vice President responsible for EPCOT for Walt Disney World Company.

Christine Robins, President & CEO of Char-Broil, LLC, the privately held manufacturer of charcoal, gas and electric outdoor grills, smokers and related equipment and former two-time global CEO.

Greg Roth, former CEO of several publicly traded companies

Steve Schneider, Managing Director at Wintrust Commercial Banking and former Managing Partner of Blackman Kallick (now Plante Moran) in Chicago.

Kyle Seymour, President of S&C Electric, Inc., a global specialist in electric power switching and protection products and services, and former Chairman, President, and CEO of Xtek, Inc.

David Smith, former President and CEO of The MOREY Corporation, a privately held enterprise, plus a four-time CEO with publicly traded companies.

Adrienne Stevens, former President of Notions Marketing Corporation, one of the largest arts and crafts supplies distributors in the U.S., and former president of L-3 Communications Avionics Systems, Inc.

Diane Strong, President and Owner of Manpower of WV, Inc.

Mark Wildman, former Chief Marketing Officer of The Parking Spot, a roll-up of 34 off-airport parking facilities.

Sam Zietz, CEO of TouchSuite, a leading provider of point of sale systems from small to mid-size retailers, and an E&Y Entrepreneur of the Year in 2015 in Florida.

The leaders who were the focus of the blog posts written after the first edition of the book was published:

- *Hardik Bhatt*, former Chief Digital Officer & State (of Illinois) CIO

- *Craig Duchossois*, Chairman and CEO of The Duchossois Group, Inc.

- *Paul Darley*, President & CEO of W.S. Darley & Co

- *Kim Feil*, board member, Chief Marketing & Strategy Officer of Aspire Healthy Energy Drinks

- *Travis Johnson*, former Co-Founder and CEO of foodjunky.com

- *Joe Poehling*, CEO of First Supply LLC.

- *Bryan Schwartz*, President of Trim-Tex, Inc.

- *Brian Scudamore*, Founder & CEO of 1-800-GOT-JUNK? & O2E

- *Michael Small*, former President & CEO of Gogo Inc.

- *Rosemary Sweirk*, President of Direct Steel and Construction

- *Ed Wehmer*, President & CEO of Wintrust Financial Corp.

Our clients, the groups we've addressed and the attendees of our workshops.

And most importantly, Elizabeth, my wife, who has been a source of constant support and understanding throughout the process. She had put up with more than usual on this one.

Lee Eisenstaedt
May 2019

Table of Contents

Foreword 1

Background 3

Chapter 1 - The Quest for Self-Awareness 9

Chapter 2 - Culture is the Catalyst 23

Chapter 3 - Get Better Answers That Move The Needle 37

Chapter 4 - Focus on Fewer and Bigger 51

Chapter 5 - Delegate, Automate, Do, or Eliminate 63

Chapter 6 - Foster Trust and Alignment 77

Chapter 7 - Identify Your High Performing Team – Part I 85

Chapter 8 - Identify Your High Performing Team – Part II 103

Chapter 9 - Be Open to Innovation and Novelty 111

Chapter 10 - Craft A Winning Strategy 123

Chapter 11 - Bringing It All Together 133

Foreword

In my experience working with business leaders, clients, other lawyers, boards of directors, and executives and college coaches in the tennis world, it often seems that self-awareness separates the good from the great and those who struggle to make an impact as opposed to those who embrace and inspire others and excel.

I first met Lee Eisenstaedt a few years ago as part of his research for another book on leadership. As long as I have known Lee, he has been an advocate for increasing one's self-awareness with respect to both one's leadership strengths and limitations. Lee believes that it is a never-ending journey whose rewards include remaining relevant, improving the lives of those with whom we are privileged to work and serve, and self-actualizing.

When I reflect on the people I have known who are the most self-aware, they have never hesitated to seek out the opinions of others, especially when those opinions are different from their own. Indeed, self-aware leaders embrace diversity of thought and perspective when they are brainstorming and making key decisions. They do not shrink to have intelligent, outspoken voices in the room who see the world through a different prism. In addition, self-aware leaders proactively and regularly ask, "What can we/I be doing better?" and "What do you think?" It takes courage to ask these questions. In my experience, it is one of the reasons that self-aware leaders have been able to make a difference in their chosen fields, be they the likes of law, business, technology, medicine, or sport.

I have also learned that, when we combine self-awareness with vision, talent, humility, and vulnerability, we can create a winning formula for inspiring and leading others and setting the bar high for achievement. Removing any of these elements from the mix seems to diminish our ability to make a lasting, genuine impact - but self-awareness is the critical component.

The foregoing skills are especially necessary in the hyper-speed world we now live. As our situations and needs change, we have to adapt and grow. Sometimes what worked in the past will work again, but it is more likely that we will need to make adjustments or change course. Sometimes those refinements are obvious. Nevertheless, I have found that, despite good intentions or vast experience, the good counsel of others almost invariably identifies more alternatives, leads to better decision-making, and creates greater engagement with those with whom we collaborate.

Of course, keeping an open mind can be challenging. So can seeing things from other people's perspectives. So can having the courage to suggest an idea that we may not have crystallized, that may need shoring up, or that may simply fall flat. When, however, we do these things, and when we take a genuine interest in what others are thinking and sharing, the results are usually more significant.

Yes, technical skills and high levels of competence are vital. They go without saying. To be an effective and engaging leader, more is required. This includes emotional intelligence, being curious, practicing active listening, following through on commitments, and giving honest, respectful, and timely feedback, just to name a few. All of us can improve on these items. We must remind ourselves never to rest on our laurels or to take things or others for granted.

Whether you are an emerging or an experienced leader, Lee's book contains wise counsel, practical advice, and critical reminders of leadership fundamentals. For those who aspire to broader, more complex roles, the insights and proven tools and processes Lee shares in his book, and through the Leading With Courage Academy, can reduce the stress of our individual journeys and increase the likelihood we will succeed. Perhaps more importantly, they can enhance our self-awareness.

Jon Vegosen

Co-Founder of Chicago-based law firm,
Funkhouser Vegosen Liebman & Dunn Ltd.

Chairman of the Board of the
Intercollegiate Tennis Association

Past Chairman of the Board, President,
and CEO of the United States Tennis Association

May 2019

Background

*"Courage is resistance to fear, mastery of
fear – not absence of fear."*
Mark Twain

In this book, you will find nine blind spots that contribute to 40% -
50% of C-level executives failing, being pushed out or quitting within the
first 18 months of starting their jobs.[1] You will discover bits of wisdom
from 40 executives who have successfully navigated the first year and
one half in their roles, including what they did to avoid, minimize and/or
recover from some or all of these obstacles.

This is a collection of best practices and tips for leaders and managers
who want to make more significant impacts on their businesses by
motivating and retaining their employees and creating more engaged,
higher-performing organizations. It is also intended to help newly
appointed execs take advantage of the time prior to their start date and
during the early days on the job. Using that time to develop an
understanding of their new environment, strategic imperatives,
customers, key business partners, employees and organizational
capabilities to help ensure they are successful. By not falling behind the
learning curve, newly appointed executives and board members can
avoid some of the obstacles that can impede their transition.

This book has also been written for managers who are leading teams
or departments and may, or may not, aspire to more complex, challenging
roles. Regardless of where they are on the organization chart and where
they want to go on it, the insights found in this book will help them be
more effective at improving communication, teamwork, and productivity.

It is also intended to augment the work done by many executive
coaches and recruiters to help newly placed executives be successful in
their roles. It should be considered a complement to books such as *The
First 90 Days* by Michael Watkins.

The 40 executives interviewed for this book and companion blog,
confirmed my own experience and hypothesis going into it – that leaders
and managers face similar issues regardless of their position, industry,
age, race and gender. Their core issues are the same, but how they tackle
them is dictated by their unique situations.

By being aware of these insights, it is my hope that you will:

- Successfully navigate your path to success,
- Create your role, not just fill it,
- Be better positioned to seize your leadership moment,
- Be the type of person you would want to work for, and
- Make an impact faster that's even bigger than expected.

To help you understand what drives my passion for helping leaders and managers, what motivated me to write this book and why I created a firm that focuses on this, let me share with you how I started on my journey.

Summer 1997

My request to attend the Center for Creative Leadership's (CCL) signature Leadership Development Program was approved. This program is an intense, five-day program of personalized feedback and self-discovery using a variety of exercises, coaches and observers, and validated assessment tools built around six factors vital to the success of managers: influence, communication, thinking and acting systemically, self-awareness, resiliency, and learning agility.

The last day of the program included a half-day, one-on-one session with a psychologist to understand and interpret the insights from my self- and 360 assessments, exercises, and observer feedback that was gathered during the four previous days. Among the blind spots that were identified was how I was not comfortable sharing with others my career goals, thinking it was shameless self-promotion. I was advised that if I wanted to get to where I wanted to go, I would have to get past this.

My goal was a second international assignment. So, I started to meet with people who made decisions about filling these assignments including the VP of Finance for Europe, the company's Chief Financial Officer, several country managers, and several people who were in the type of position I wanted. While I made it clear to each person what I was interested in, the conversations centered around what experience or projects I should seek out that would make me a better fit for them, what it takes to be successful in the roles, etc.

At first, I felt awkward talking about myself, but each conversation got easier. I quickly saw that what I was doing was building awareness of me among decision makers and doing it in ways that I shouldn't be ashamed of or think were a sign of bad upbringing.

My investment in CCL paid off. In spring 1998 I was offered the assignment I had dreamed of in Paris, France. I'm sure it wouldn't have been extended to me had I not discovered one of my blind spots and then committed myself to overcoming it.

Now to the next part of this journey.

June 1998

I had just arrived in Paris on a three-year assignment with SC Johnson, the maker of Windex® and Pledge®, as the Finance Director for five countries – France, Spain, Portugal, Belgium and Holland. This was my second assignment in France. My wife Elizabeth and I had signed a three-year lease for an apartment in a Belle Époque building just two blocks from where we had lived four years prior and one half of a mile west of the Arc de Triomphe.

We had kept the bank account we opened at Societe Generale at the start of our first assignment. We knew the days the local outdoor market was held (Wednesdays and Sundays) and where to shop when it wasn't. We knew how to use the Metro and buses. We even qualified to exchange our Illinois driver's licenses for French licenses for just 1 euro without having to take the otherwise obligatory six-month long driving class in French that cost about 800 euros. We would be able to go to our favorite neighborhood restaurants, knew where to get our hair cut and, most importantly, be with our French friends, beginning Day One.

Since my first assignment in France lasted less than one year, no one described us as being fluent in French. In fact, neither Elizabeth nor I had studied the language before relocating to Paris. Because we were committed to integrating into our new surroundings, Elizabeth enrolled in language classes at the Sorbonne and I studied French at Berlitz. We also wanted to understand the culture. To do so, we preferred being with the locals to other Americans. This was the right thing to have done, but it had the unintended consequence of creating some resentment towards us by many of the IBM expatriates in our building.

About one week into the assignment, our household goods arrived from the U.S. and by the end of the third week, we had unpacked everything. Elizabeth, Chloe (our standard poodle) and I were quickly settling into our new surroundings. One great pleasure was taking coffee in the mornings at the café near our apartment with Chloe while reading *The International Herald Tribune* and *Le Figaro* and sharing a croissant. Another was dining out, which Elizabeth and I did at least three evenings each week. Sometimes Chloe accompanied us, as it seemed that dogs were more welcome in restaurants than children.

Six weeks into the assignment and all was going well. I was getting to know my boss, who was also my sponsor and mentor, my team and the operations assigned to me. I was learning the language and about the culture. Before moving to Paris, we had sold our house and cars and Elizabeth had resigned from her position. We were committed to this move and did not want to give anyone a reason to cut the assignment short.

Then, a seismic change occurred at work.

Just six weeks after starting in the role, my boss announced he was leaving the company -- the next day.

During my drive home, I repeatedly role-played how I would break the news to Elizabeth. I also tried to remember what, if any, signals there had been that my boss would leave so soon and without any notice. Like all Black Swan events, the indicators were obvious only after the fact.

When I told Elizabeth about the situation at work, she told me that like Hernán Cortés, the Spanish conquistador five centuries ago, we had "*burned our boats*" and had no Plan B. She went on to tell me in a calm and firm voice how my only choice was "*...to make this work.*" Then we went out to dinner to develop a strategy.

Beginning the next day, I doubled down on understanding how the business worked, knowing my team and learning the language and culture. I learned how the company grew, how its products were differentiated from others in the market and how it earned its profits. I learned what had been done before I arrived that got the group to where it was at that time and what was working. I also identified perceptions, misalignments and assumptions that needed attention and clarity. I built new networks inside and outside the company and sought out the advice of others who had found themselves in similar situations.

All of this work paid off.

- I became a trusted advisor and resource to my new boss and the one that succeeded him two years later.

- I learned the language to the point that I was comfortable delivering a 15-minute speech, entirely in French, to 150 employees on the state of the company. I not only did this six months into the assignment, but every six months thereafter.

- I led several significant projects, including the conversion to the Euro and preparing the company for the Millennium, as well as moving back office operations to a shared services center in the UK. The first two were a particular challenge because no one had ever done anything like them before. This meant there were no "best practice" road maps to follow.

- I championed the implementation of a holistic sales and operations planning process, guided a major product recall, consolidated outside legal counsel into one firm, reorganized our logistics network and restructured the groups I oversaw to reflect the new realities of our business.

These successes contributed to the five countries to which I was assigned being among the most profitable in the company's European division. Our leadership team came to be respected by our peers within and outside the company who regularly sought out our insights and perspectives. Most surrealistic of all was that by the end of my four-year assignment, the local French employees were asking me where they should go in Paris for dinner.

I had stuck the landing.

France was a game changer for Elizabeth and me. It broadened our perspectives and outlook. It allowed me to hone my skill of learning new business models and cultures and applying that understanding to address challenging issues and solve complex problems. The experience also improved my communication, people, leadership and project management skills. It gave me the confidence necessary to change industries when I retired from SC Johnson and to start my own business – twice. And as Elizabeth is quick to remind me, "everything since Paris has been downhill." Not really, but she makes a point of how great a time we had there.

Now, I hope that between this book and the Leading With Courage Academy's assessments, workshops, and coaching, that I'm able to help others find peace of mind and be more confident by:

- More clearly understanding themselves and how others see them,

- Being aware of their leadership blind spots so they're neither surprised by nor a victim of them

- Identifying these blind spots earlier in their careers,

- Summoning the courage to move outside of their comfort zones to elevate their performance and achievements,

- Pre-empting the dysfunctional behaviors that unknowingly inhibit their growth and their ability to motivate and retain team members, and

- Leveraging the tools, processes and insights, successes, and mistakes I've acquired over more than 35 years of being coached, attending development programs, onboarding, integrating and continuous learning.

[1]Heidrick & Struggles International and The Corporate Executive Board

Chapter 1

The Quest for Self-Awareness

*Don't accept your dog's admiration as
conclusive evidence that you are wonderful."*
Ann Landers

The overarching theme of this book is self-awareness. It's about having the courage to identify and tackle your leadership blind spots, primarily by asking others what they think and what could you be doing better or differently. If you are reluctant to ask these sorts of questions, then I fear you will be disappointed by what follows.

Self-awareness of our limitations, biases and blind spots enables leaders and managers to work with others who have strengths and opinions different than their own. Self-awareness allows us to more readily accept the possibility that someone else may have a better idea or different way of doing things. A lack of self-awareness can alienate others by misunderstanding the impact our emotions, behaviors, and decisions have on them.

While high self-awareness has been found to be one of the strongest predictors of overall success (Cornell University, School of Industrial and Labor Relations, 2010), it eludes most of us. According to Dr. Tasha Eurich, an organizational psychologist, researcher, and New York Times best-selling author, 95% of people claim to be self-aware, while the real number is only 12% - 15%.

In our practice, for example, our biggest competitors are not other consultants or coaches. It's the leaders and managers we encounter who see themselves as being self-aware when they are not. It's made worse by those who think they know themselves the best are often the least self-aware.

Self-awareness is hard work. It's an ongoing process of self-reflection that requires regularly checking in with yourself and others to see where you are at, how others perceive you, and what your current strengths and limitations are. It's about understanding where your biases and preferences lie and knowing how you can overcome them so you can make the impact you want to make. It's about being authentic with yourself and others, being vulnerable, being able to admit you're wrong and open to changing your behavior.

It is not something gained by a one-time personality assessment taken 20 years ago that categorized you as a series of letters or put you into a box on a grid.

It is about striving to improve and to understand that where you are at and how you're thinking has been influenced by all of the all the experiences you have had, the beliefs you have formed, and the opinions you hold. Self-awareness is having a realistic view of your strengths, limitations, thoughts, beliefs, motivation and emotions.

It requires you to honestly answer these four questions each time someone provides you with feedback or a situation doesn't align with what you expected or wanted:

- What am I willing to let go of?
- What am I willing to give up?
- What am I willing to take responsibility for?
- What am I willing to forgive another or myself for?

In some cases, your answers to each of these questions will be "nothing." And these may be the right answers to each of them. I think that case may define a "fall on your sword" issue or challenge, which is okay, as long as you're prepared to accept the intended and unintended consequences of it.

Self-awareness allows you to more clearly understand yourself and how others see you. And because situations and circumstances are changing all the time, you can never be totally self-aware for very long, if ever. Hence, self-awareness is a life-long journey.

The End in Mind is Improving Your Self-Awareness

The goal of this book and the Leading With Courage Academy is to help you increase your emotional and social awareness, discover your leadership blind spots and strengths, and to help you manage your responses to situations more effectively.

Feedback, training and in-the-job development are crucial to discovering your need for changes and stretching yourself. However, as you reach more senior levels in an organization there may be fewer opportunities for honest feedback and positive development as you are viewed as competent and not in need of support by others and frequently yourself. But, don't believe your own press clippings, rest on your laurels, or wait to be surprised by your blind spots.

Along these lines, there's a great story told by George C. Scott in the 1970 movie *Patton*:

> *For over a thousand years, Roman conquerors returning from the wars enjoyed the honor of a triumph - a tumultuous parade. In the procession came trumpeters and musicians and strange animals from the conquered territories, together with carts laden with treasure and captured armaments. The conqueror rode in a triumphal chariot, the dazed prisoners walking in chains before him. Sometimes his children, robed in white, stood with him in the chariot, or rode the trace horses. A slave stood behind the conqueror, holding a golden crown, and whispering in his ear a warning: that all glory is fleeting.*

But so often we hear leaders, especially those in the C-Suite, tell us something like: "*I don't need this. That's why I'm the CEO.*" It's as if they had been hit by a ray gun that made them totally self-aware by virtue of having been promoted to the top spot.

Outside of their self-created, self-empowering and self-reinforcing perspective of themselves and the world, they overlook their peers, bosses, direct reports, suppliers, service providers, customers, and coaches who can foresee things that can happen to them before they actually occur. They are able to do this based on the elements in front of them – the people, the environment, the vision, the goals, the experience of others, etc. They can see that integrations are going to be difficult if relationships aren't built quickly. They can see when leaders and managers don't accept the wisdom of others from a peer advisory board, mastermind group or 360 feedback, they risk becoming the problem. They can recognize arrogance and zero self-awareness when they hear "*Fix these people. They're the ones with the problems and blind spots. Not me.*"

It reminds me of the story in Greek mythology of the prophetess Cassandra. Apollo gifted Cassandra with the power to foretell great prophecies that would come true, but she was simultaneously cursed in that nobody ever believed these prophecies. No matter what she said or did, regardless if facts and experience were on her side, no one would believe her.

The Nine BEHAVIORS of Leading With Courage

The choice of the word "behaviors" in the sub-title of this book over values, norms, beliefs, and assumptions was deliberate. We can see behaviors, whereas it is hard, if not impossible, to observe those other ideas because they exist only in a world of language. Our behaviors are partly shaped by our norms, beliefs, morals, etc., and as such are the physical embodiment of them. We chose "behaviors" because we have a preference for the tangible and practical to the highly abstract and academic, which is another theme throughout this book and at the Leading With Courage Academy.

According to Genos International, one of Training Industry, Inc.'s Top 20 Assessment and Evaluation Companies in 2018, our behaviors are shaped by our emotions, which in turn influence our decisions and performance, in both productive and unproductive ways. It's also known that there's a direct link between the way we feel and the way we perform at work.

Genos also observes that in high-performing organizations, people feel significantly more engaged, cared for, valued, proud, and motivated than those in lower-performing organizations. Conversely, in low performing workplaces, people feel substantially more fearful, stressed, disempowered and uncertain. We believe that everyone deserves to work for engaged, high-performing leaders in engaged high-performing organizations.

Emotional Intelligence

Because leadership is fundamentally about getting others to perform, Genos (and the Leading With Courage Academy) believes effective leaders need to be skilled at identifying, understanding and managing emotions in themselves and others to drive optimal decisions, behavior and performance. This skill is called emotional intelligence (EI) and when it's applied to leadership, it's about how intelligently you use emotions to get positive results.

> *(In the interest of full-disclosure, the Leading With Courage Academy is a certified Genos International EI practitioner.*

This means we are authorized to offer for sale the Genos suite of self-, 180-, and 360-assessments and workshops.)

Research has proven that a leader's emotional intelligence is directly linked to their ability to drive high performance and employee engagement. It is also correlated with leadership ability and separates good from great performers. Here are some examples of the benefits EI:

- According to TalentSmart, 90% of top performers are also high in emotional intelligence. On the flip side, just 20% of bottom performers are high in emotional intelligence.

- Research by the Center for Creative Leadership (CCL) found that the primary causes of executive derailment involve deficiencies in emotional competence

- 90% of what moves people up the ladder when IQ and technical skills are similar is emotional intelligence per the Harvard Business Review.

- In a 2011 Career Builder Survey of more than 2,600 hiring managers and human resource professionals, 71% stated they valued emotional intelligence in an employee over IQ; 75% said they were more likely to promote a highly emotionally intelligent worker; and 59% claimed they'd pass up a candidate with a high IQ but low emotional intelligence.

- In one of McDonalds' suppliers in Europe, almost half of managers' performance (47%) was predicted just by emotional intelligence scores (Hay Group).

- A study of over 40 Fortune 500 companies revealed that salespeople with high Emotional Intelligence outperformed those with medium to low EI by 50% (Expedite Consulting).

To help you more quickly grasp what EI looks like, the chart on the next page shows 13 behaviors of people with high emotional intelligence.

Thirteen Behaviors Consistent With High Emotional Intelligence

You think about feelings EI starts here	**You pause** You refrain from making a permanent decision or impression based on a temporary emotion	**You strive to control your thoughts** You're not a slave to your emotions	**You benefit from criticism** You ask. How can this make me better?
You show authenticity You say what you mean and mean what you say	**You demonstrate empathy** Empathy doesn't mean agreement	**You praise others** To build trust and alignment	**You give helpful feedback** Both the good and the bad
You apologize Valuing relationships more than your ego	**You forgive and forget** This allows you to move forward	**You keep your commitments** This develops your reputation for reliability and trustworthiness	**You help others** Most people don't care about where you graduated from or your previous accomplishments

You protect yourself from emotional sabotage

If you would like a shorter list of high-EI traits, here are six attributes:

1. You can deal with the stresses and pressures at work in a healthy, productive manner
2. You understand and cooperate with others
3. You're a good listener
4. You seek and are open to feedback
5. You are empathetic; you can put your own emotions and desires aside to take others into account
6. You set an example for others to follow

Unlike IQ, emotional intelligence can change over time based on the company and culture you're working in, your role in an organization, personal events such as falling in and out of love, the birth of a child, and the loss of a parent, your health, and any number of other factors. This is why we encourage our clients to regularly seek feedback from others on their demonstration of core EI competencies that include self-awareness, awareness of others, authenticity, and inspiring performance. And as was touched on above, you can improve your impact, influence, and resilience as a leader by developing your emotional intelligence skills through learning, practice, and assessments.

Another reason for embracing EI is because it's a powerful language and set of behaviors that enable you to make a difference that's not dependent on the others with whom you work being overly familiar with the language nor agile practitioners of the behaviors. Your development will be greater, and you'll progress faster when the people around you have a shared understanding of EI, but this not essential and necessary for you to make a difference.

This is different from the DiSC behavioral assessment.

DiSC

DiSC is a behavioral assessment that helps you understand yourself and others so you can improve communication, productivity and teamwork. It was developed by William Moulton Marston in the late 1920s and validated during his studies at Harvard University. He later defined the four quadrants of personality as Dominance, Inclusion, Steadiness, and Conscientiousness. Then in 1940, Walter Clark took Marston's theory and developed the first DISC behavior profile as we know it today. Since John Wiley & Sons started to invest in the tool it markets as Everything DiSC®□, the assessment has been taken:

- By more than 7,000,000 people,
- In over 100,000 organization, and
- In more than 70 countries and in least 12 languages.

(Again, to be fully transparent, Leading With Courage Academy is an authorized partner of Everything DiSC®.)

Since there is already a lot of material available on DiSC, we will only briefly describe each of the four styles, of which there are 12 sub-styles.

- **Dominance**: A person with a "D" style places emphasis on accomplishing results, the bottom line, and confidence. They are commonly described as direct, demanding, forceful, strong willed, driven, determined, fast-paced, and self-confident. They value competency, action, concrete results, personal freedom, and challenges. They may be limited by a lack of concern for others and impatience and may fear being seen as vulnerable or being taken advantage of.

- **Influence**: An "I" emphasizes influencing or persuading others, openness, and relationships. They are usually described as convincing, magnetic, enthusiastic, warm, trusting and optimistic. Their priorities include taking action, collaboration, and expressing enthusiasm, and are motivated by social recognition and group activities. I's may fear loss of influence, disapproval and being ignored, and value coaching and counseling, freedom of expression and democratic relationships. Strong I's may be limited by being impulsive, disorganized and having a lack of follow-through.

- **Steadiness**: Those with an "S" style have a preference for cooperation, sincerity, and dependability. They are motivated by opportunities to help and sincere appreciation, and have as their priorities giving support, collaborating and maintaining stability. S's are usually described as calm, patient, predictable, deliberate, stable and consistent and may be limited by being indecisive, overly accommodating, and satisfied with the status quo. While they may fear change, loss of stability, and offending others, they value loyalty, helping others and security.

- **Conscientiousness**: C's place emphasis on quality and accuracy, expertise and competency. Individuals with a C-style are likely to be motivated by opportunities to gain knowledge, show their expertise, and produce quality work, while prioritizing ensuring accuracy, maintaining stability, and challenging assumptions. They are frequently described as careful, cautious, systematic, diplomatic, accurate and tactful and may be limited by being overly critical, overanalyzing and isolating themselves as they fear criticism and being wrong.

EI And DiSC Are Complementary And Not Substitutes

We are advocates of taking multiple behavior assessments because while there is usually some overlap among them, together they validate insights they've each revealed which contributes to building a more complete, multi-dimensional profile of what makes you, you.

Here are several things to keep in mind with EI and DiSC:

- We find that DiSC makes the most impact when the people you work with are familiar with the tool and have an awareness of their own style, or in the language of Everything DiSC, where their "dot" is. Without this shared understanding, it's a bit like being on a desert island or trying to play tennis or baseball all by yourself. It's tough to accomplish a lot. We don't find this to be the case with EI. While the ideal situation is for everyone you work with to be familiar with their own EI strengths and limitations, you can accomplish a lot if you are the only person in the group who is fluent in EI's language and behaviors.

- DiSC, unlike EI, tends to remain the same over time. It's also based on a self-assessment, while we find you are best measuring how you're perceived by asking others for feedback using a 180- or 360-assessment.

- DiSC style is not a "predictor" of success. Any DiSC style can succeed in any position. This is why DiSC should not be used as the basis for hiring or promoting someone. This is in contrast to EI which among its assessments has one specifically designed for evaluating candidates from outside the organization.

- While DiSC may be a "nice to know" about someone being considered for a promotion, that same candidate's level of EI is more of a "need to know" because of its linkage to leadership and the ability to create engaged, highly-performing organizations. With that in mind, *EI should account for no more than one-third of the factors that go into making a hiring or promotion decision.*

- There are no comparisons to a norm group of the general population with DiSC. EI provides these, which is one reason it's useful in making hiring and promotion decisions. The comparison to norm groups is also helpful when deciding which of several areas of concern to focus on improving.

- One of the most significant advantages of Everything DiSC compared to EI is how it allows users of the tool to run comparison reports between themselves and anyone else who has taken the assessment. These are 10-page reports that compare people on six different competencies and provide insights into what motivates and stresses each person, their communication preferences, and how best to work together. We find that the comparison reports offer a solid foundation from which to have a structured, consistent, and intentional conversation with a new boss, direct report, or client. While some people fear sharing so much information, the reality is both of you will discover all of this about the other over a period of months. So, why not jump-start the process of building greater productivity, communication and teamwork as soon as possible?

We also prefer DiSC to Myers Briggs, the other well-known behavior profile, because we find DiSC easier to understand, communicate, and use. Both are good, but when given a choice between them, we lean into the tool that's more practical for most people and situations.

Three Exercises to **Build Your Courage Muscles**

➢ **Take a 180- or 360-assessment of your emotional intelligence.** Arrange to solicit anonymous, confidential feedback from others on your strengths and limitations. This is preferred to a self-assessment, which is limited to your impressions of yourself and prone to positive bias. Knowing how you "show up" according to others is a much more accurate reading of how you are perceived and action oriented. If you do not already have a preferred supplier for these sorts of assessments, please contact the Leading With Courage Academy.

➢ **Start to keep a journal or diary** in which you regularly reflect on the way you are thinking, feeling and acting at work. Note the impact your emotions are having on others.

➢ **Take a DiSC behavioral assessment** to identify your own style, and an ability to read the personality types of the people with whom you work. Again, if you do not already have a preferred provider, please reach out to the Leading With Courage Academy, which is an authorized partner of Everything DiSC®.

Take Aways to **Be Leading With Courage**

At the end of each chapter, I'll provide you with several key take-aways to remember and establish as part of your process. Here's our first set.

> ➤ Being self-aware is a hallmark of great leaders and managers, but it is hard work and requires a life-long commitment to learning and change.

> ➤ Every leader or manager with real courage has to possess the self-awareness and humility to acknowledge their own strengths and limitations as well as those of their team where applicable. It's a must if you want to keep the momentum of your career and organization moving forward and to stay relevant and competitive.

> ➤ Having the courage to ask others "how am I doing" and "what can I do better" is perhaps the best way to improve your self-awareness. Listening to what you're told and being open to making some changes is essential too.

> ➤ Multiple assessments should be used to develop a fully-informed understanding of your strengths, limitations, preferences, and tendencies. Everything DiSC and Genos Emotional Intelligence are but two of the research-based, validated, and proven assessments and theoretical constructs available to help you on your journey.

Notes

Notes

Chapter 2

Culture is the Catalyst

"Culture eats strategy for breakfast."
Peter Drucker

Culture is the first behavior discussed for a reason – not paying sufficient attention to culture is the most frequently cited blind spot a newly appointed executive must avoid, minimize or recover from.

Each of the 25 C-level execs interviewed for this book said that an organization's culture must be understood, honored, and respected if he or she is to be successful. At best, failing to do so leads to winning strategies sitting on the shelf. At worst, it is the equivalent of a transplanted organ being rejected by the body – the host's antibodies rally to do whatever is required to maintain the status quo. When this occurs, the leader or manager fails, is pushed out or quits.

This happens to 40% - 50% of newly appointed executives within the first 18 months of filling their positions.[1]

> *An organization's culture is a powerful differentiator and a source of competitive advantage. Taking the time to understand what owners, leaders and employees are most proud of about their organizations, what makes them want to come to work each day, and what drives them to go beyond expectations is a prerequisite for shifting a culture.*

What Culture Is and Is Not

Let's agree on the following: An organization's culture is not like a hand of five-card stud poker – you can't easily exchange the cards you've been dealt for new ones. Nor is culture a used car that you can simply trade in for a newer model with better gas mileage, updated styling and no dents, dings or squeaks.

With that as our understanding of what culture is not, here's our definition of what an organization's culture is: **Culture is your company's operating system and the engine that drives your results.**

Culture is also:

- Shared beliefs, values and assumptions
- Embedded in the organizational practices
- How things get done on a day-to-day basis
- Visible in the behaviors of groups and individuals
- Amplified by the behaviors of leaders

Two things to keep in mind:

- Your organization's culture is defined by the worst behavior your leaders accept.
- If you have just one employee, then you have a culture.

In chemistry, a catalyst is a substance that causes or accelerates a chemical reaction without itself being affected. Culture has similar properties. It promotes or enables a significant change or action and it doesn't change in the process. Culture can also hinder progress too.

By leveraging the best points of an organization's culture, you can offset or mitigate the impact of its most negative aspects. But completely overhauling an organization's culture? Sorry. That's nearly impossible. The most skilled leaders should only attempt it in the direst of circumstances after all other efforts to modify it have failed.

Again, the key words here are *mitigate* and *modify*. Not overhaul. Your chances for success will be greater when you try to work with what you have to affect the kind of change you want.

Discovering the Culture

To shift a company's culture, you first need to observe, talk to and survey a lot people at all levels of the organization. In doing so, you begin to learn about its values, history and accomplishments.

Even when you think you know the culture, you may not. Consider this story from Kyle Seymour, President of S&C Electric, a global, electric power switching and protection products and services company.

Prior to moving into his current position, Kyle had been on the board of directors of the company for about two years. Consequently, with all the knowledge he'd obtained, Kyle was confident that he understood the culture of the company and its hot buttons.

He quickly learned there was an unwritten cultural norm he hadn't heard about – a behavioral norm so ingrained in S&C's culture that it wasn't written down anywhere. It was assumed to be a given and was taken for granted. But someone coming into the company from outside of it, like Kyle, wouldn't be aware of it.

The behavioral norm Kyle discovered was that you don't take vacation days during certain times of the year. Especially when you're as visible as the President of the company. Violating this norm threw some people into shock, but the practice was only revealed when Kyle actually stepped on this blind spot.

When we help our clients with this at Leading With Courage Academy, we don't ask their employees to "describe the company's values." Really, why would we? All we're likely to hear in response are vague terms like integrity, customer-centricity, quality, innovation and professionalism. These are examples of ideas that only exist in the world of language and nearly every organization names these qualities.

Go ahead – make a list of your company's values and then describe them. On a scale from one to ten, *how easy was that?*

Instead, let's ask a question that is easier to answer and provides deeper, more tangible insights: *"What is not tolerated around here?"* Let's follow it up with one of our most favorite questions: *"Anything else?"*

Keep asking this until there's nothing more that comes to mind. What is considered a violation of your organization's culture? Anything else?

Sam Zietz, founder and CEO of TouchSuite, a company in Boca Raton, Florida that solves the payment processing problems of smaller retailers, shared with me his company's values. What I found unique and memorable about them is they are tangible behaviors that clearly convey what is expected of everyone working at the company.

Have a look at TouchSuite's criteria below and you'll see what I mean:

Always have a sense of urgency	Create market disruption
Seek constant improvement	Have fun
Every problem has a solution...find it	No excuses
Act with integrity	Act like an owner
Always exceed expectations	

Compare TouchSuite's list to the values you'll find on practically every national professional services firm's website: Respect, Excellence, Integrity, Teamwork and Stewardship. Which do you find easier to understand, model and communicate to others?

Listen to Learn, Learn to Listen

When talking to employees, listen closely to the stories they tell about the company's history, accomplishments and people.

In 1983, Stanford professor Joanne Martin led a group of researchers that identified seven common types of stories that are good indicators of an organization's culture[2].

These seven cultural indicators are:

1. ***Is the big boss human?*** This story is about an authority figure – a leader, manager or founder – who has the opportunity to show that he or she is better than everyone else and how they behave.

2. ***Can a little person rise to the top?*** The plot is the basic Horatio Alger, rags to riches story.

3. ***Will I get fired?*** These are stories about what happens when times are tough. Does the company fire or lay off employees?

4. ***How will the boss react to mistakes?*** These are the tales about what happens when someone makes a mistake. Do they get fired, humiliated in front of others or do they get a second chance?

5. ***Will the organization help me when I have to move?*** The central character of these stories is an employee who is moved repeatedly from office to office or city to city. The plot revolves around the difficulties they face and how the company helps them and their family.

6. ***What happens when a boss is caught breaking a rule?*** These stories involve two people – one is a high-status person while the other is a subordinate

and frequently a new hire. The high-status person is caught breaking a company rule and the low-status person points this out to him or her. How did the high-status person react to being challenged?

7. ***How will the organization deal with obstacles?*** These are the most common stories. They deal with obstacles that are internal to the organization, external to it or technical in nature. Do people go above and beyond their job descriptions to deal with problems? Or are they passive, preferring to adhere to standard operating procedures?

If you look closely at the seven stories, you'll see they can be grouped into three distinct themes.

- The first is **justice**: Is this a fair place?

- Next is **security**: Is it safe to work here?

- The third is **control**: Can I shape my destiny and have influence in this organization?

If the study was conducted today, it's likely there would also be stories about innovation, work / life balance, respect, and equal opportunity. It's also likely that these new stories would be subsets of the seven listed above.

Surveys Are Useful

Where do you begin to understand the attitudes of your organization's employees?

You can start by purchasing or designing an electronic survey sent to all of your employees. One advantage of these surveys is that their results are comparable across departments, subsidiaries and time. When these surveys are followed up with focus groups composed of 6-10 employees, you can really dive into specific issues to address.

In fact, the approach of surveys combined with focus groups is one we use at the start of nearly all of our consulting assignments at Leading With Courage Academy.

It is quite common for our engagements to begin with three assessments:

- Culture
- High-performing organization
- Employee engagement

These are accompanied by face-to-face conversations with leaders and other key employees. After all the data is gathered and analyzed, we have much better insights into an organization's culture, what's working well, what isn't, and what the employees need from their leaders and managers to do their jobs better. This allows us to identify and prioritize with our client the areas that need to be addressed.

For surveys of employee attitudes to be an effective tool for shifting the culture, you'll want to keep the following in mind:

- **You must be committed to following up on results you receive.** Asking employees for their feedback will raise their expectations that something will be changed. If you're not going to do something with the results, don't spend the time and money conducting the surveys.

- **Focus on a few things to change.** Pick three or four initiatives and after making significant, visible progress on them, pick two or three more to work on.

- **Communicate on progress being made in implementing change.** Bring this to life by sharing stories of people who have adopted the new behaviors and the impact it has had on their teams, customers, the company and/or the communities you serve. Better yet, have these people tell their stories at employee meetings and make videos of them that can be posted on your website.

You'll also want to select measures that are easy to track and communicate. The simpler they are, the less complexity you'll create in the organization, the less expensive the data will be to collect and the less time you'll invest explaining what they mean to your key stakeholders. We've always found that the simpler the metrics, the higher the likelihood of implementation. If the new measures can be added to existing scorecards and reports, all the better.

Shifting the Culture

Armed with an understanding of an organization's culture, you'll be in a better position to earn your right to be seen as a change agent. You'll be able to articulate what you respect and admire about the company's culture. You'll share the stories you heard that reinforce your esteem for what has come before you arrived on the scene. And you'll have the greater insight to acknowledge all the efforts it took to get the organization to where it is today.

Christine Robins, CEO of Char-Broil LLC, the manufacturer of outdoor grills, smokers and related accessories, has done this with great success. By understanding and respecting the culture as well as knowing which aspects of that culture have to be preserved and built upon, Christine has shifted the way employees describe the company. What was once a *"conservative, internally focused, and siloed"* company is now seen as *"collaborative and consumer driven."*

In knowing what employees are most proud of and what makes them feel good about the organization, you can set your priorities and the pace at which you will tackle them. By first thinking through the impact of potential changes, you'll want to engage those who can support and implement your ideas. Enlisting their help now can avoid the unintended consequences that may accompany your change agenda.

Gay Gaddis, the founder of T3, the largest woman-owned advertising agency in the U.S., reminded me of how important is to think through the impact of taking away a benefit or some other aspect of an organization's culture. She makes a point of telling all of her teams that it is so much easier to give a benefit than to take it away and how you shouldn't do something if you aren't prepared to sustain it.

Gay told me they used to give candy away in on Fridays in their offices. At 10:30am, someone would blow a whistle and giant bowls of candy would appear. And people would come from all corners of the office to get some of it.

One year, T3 was not doing as well as planned and it had lost a major client. This prompted Gay to challenge all of their spending, including "Candy Fridays." She learned that the cost of the candy was as much as some peoples' annual salary, so she eliminated the benefit thinking she could save a lower level person's job. The reaction of the employees was swift and negative. Gay said people were screaming at her, hated her and behaved as if *"she had shot a dog in the front yard."*

The point of this story wasn't about the candy. For the employees, Candy Fridays was a symbol of loss and a tangible artifact that T3 was less fun to work at. Gay listened, of course, and restored the benefit.

Zappos, the online shoe and clothing retailer owned by Amazon, offers a great example on the importance of prioritizing its culture over business results. The company tells its employees that their values are not just suggestions – *they can actually be used as grounds for termination if they don't abide by them.*

Tony Hsieh, Zappos' CEO, has said:

> *"Our whole belief is if you get the culture right, then most of the other stuff, like delivering great customer service or building a long-term brand or business will just be a natural byproduct."*[3]

For your culture-shifting initiatives to have the greatest likelihood of being seamlessly integrated into your organization, remember to do the following:

- **Match your strategies to the culture and then be sure to repeatedly communicate how the strategies are connected to it.**

- **Choose a few behaviors to change and focus on modifying them.** Even if the changes are small, when they're adopted up, down, and across the organization, you'll be moving the needle.

- **Add or modify the mechanisms needed to reinforce the changes and encourage the desired behaviors.** You'll want to leverage both the formal and informal options for doing this. The chart below gives you an excellent sense of the differences in these options.

FORMAL	INFORMAL
<ul><li>Reporting structures</li><li>Business processes and policies</li><li>Training, leadership, and organizational development programs</li><li>Career plans and ladders</li><li>Performance management processes</li><li>Compensation systems</li><li>Internal communications</li><li>Company events and town hall meetings</li></ul>	<ul><li>Senior leaders being visible role models of new behaviors and values</li><li>Multi-functional teams and committees</li><li>Ad hoc gatherings</li><li>Storytelling</li><li>Interactions with customers and vendors</li><li>Engagement of internal opinion setters and influencers</li><li>Making changes to the physical infrastructure and aesthetics</li></ul>

Measure and monitor how the culture evolves.

Two areas to pay close attention to are:

- Changes in employee engagement and attitudes as measured through regular employee surveys

- Meeting milestones for major initiatives, keeping commitments to key accounts, implementing new policies and processes and adopting new behaviors. Some of these new behaviors could be charging for out of scope work or inputting time into the practice management system.

Now, you may have the natural urge to prioritize financial targets for measurement in the early stages, such as revenue growth and margin improvement. But I caution you against doing so. The reason being, that you want to avoid sending mixed messages. Let the attitudes and behavior changes start to take hold first. Then feel free to shift the focus in the direction of metrics that favor business performance improvement.

Let me give you an example: One of our consulting clients came to us after losing its leading market share to a key competitor. In just eight months, the company had lost 10 share points. Poof! Just like that, their advantage vanished. Clearly, the trend had to be stopped and reversed. Fortunately, the company at least realized it needed to be more customer-centric and do a much better job at satisfying the unmet and emerging needs of its customers.

With these initiatives in mind, the marketing department launched several "buy one, get one free" promotions on their most popular items. These had the effect of regaining the lost share points.

Time to celebrate, right? Not quite.

It was only a cosmetic, short-term win because the promotions led to repeat customers stocking up on 1.8 years' worth of the company's products. What's more, because the promotions were unplanned and expensive, important brand-building campaigns were cut from the marketing plan in order to meet quarterly and annual financial (and bonus) objectives. The share they'd gained was lost within a few months because the promotions for the inferior products could not be sustained and so many customers had loaded up when prices were low.

The key competitor took over the #1 position in the market a year later. It was an expensive mistake for our client to make and one we're working with them to correct so they never make it again.

[1]Heidrick & Struggles International and The Corporate Executive Board

[2]Martin, Joanne et al. "The Uniqueness Paradox in Organizational Stories". *Administrative Science Quarterly* 28.3 (1983): 438–453.

[3]Blue Sky Innovation, May 23, 2014, http://bluesky.chicagotribune.com/originals/chi-zappos-CEO-tony-hsieh-company-culture-bsi,0,0.story

Three Exercises to **Build Your Courage Muscles**

> ➤ **Learn more about your organization's culture by having face-to-face conversations with ten employees during which you ask them what they feel is a violation of your company's culture.** Choose three people from among your direct reports, four employees from the next level down from them and three people from the lowest level of the organization. Don't forget to ask them "anything else?" How similar are their perceptions?

> ➤ **Ask two employees to share their stories that demonstrate your culture at its best at your next all-employee meeting.**

> ➤ **Conduct an employee engagement survey, with a commitment to acting on what you learn.** (If you need help with this, we are big fans of the Engagement Multiplier™ platform. It is a quarterly online survey that goes to all employees and only takes 10 minutes to complete on any device. Here's a link to a short video about it: https://vimeo.com/149039960.

Take Aways to **Be Leading With Courage**

➢ When your organization's culture is already very broken and dysfunctional, it won't matter what business value enhancement strategies you bring to the table because they probably won't work.

➢ When your culture is strong and receptive, it's OK if you've chosen a strategy that's not perfect because the help will be there to fix it - as will the support you need to reach your goals and objectives.

➢ Regardless of the condition of the culture you've inherited, it's practically Mission Impossible to make *massive* shifts to it. Focus on modifying a few select behaviors at a time.

➢ The odds of successfully implementing your strategies and tactics will be much greater when you invest the time to understand, honor and respect that culture. This will better position you to leverage its strengths and offset its less desirable aspects.

➢ Communicating the reasons for the changes, why you're investing in them and what's in it for employees, customers and vendors can't be emphasized enough. It's trite, but you cannot over-communicate.

Notes

Notes

Chapter 3

Get Better Answers That Move The Needle

*"When you are an individual contributor,
you try to have all the answers. When you are
a leader, your job is to have all the questions."*
Jack Welch
Former Chairman & CEO of General Electric

When a new leader or manager comes into the organization, the expectations are so grandiose that the person might as well ride in dressed as a knight on a white horse. If you've ever joined a company in a highly visible role like this, it's not unusual to feel an air that you're going to come in and do great things from the likes of board members, employees, customers and others closely connected to the company. All the pressure is at your back. Your confidence is at an all-time high.

This is precisely when a great big ego can take over, even before actually moving into the role.

If there's one big mistake many newly appointed leader or managers make as they assume the mantle of leadership in a new company, it's that they think all situations in all companies are the same and they already know how to fix their problems. This leads them to **come in with the answer – which is the next leadership blind spot to be on the alert for.**

Yes, you've left your mark of positive results on a previous company or department, your experience is a perfect match and your education is outstanding. If you do exactly what you did at the last job in this new job, the fixes should be relatively simple, right?

Wrong, wrong, wrong.

The *"this is how we always did it there, so it should work the same here"* mentality doesn't take a lot of variables into consideration that could make the situation and outcomes profoundly different this time around.

Even if it is within the same industry, you are obviously entering a different type of company. Within that company, you will have a different culture (recall the key points of Chapter 1), different talent levels, different financial resources, different technological capabilities, different goals and more.

With so much that could be new, why would you approach it the same way as you did before? At the very least, why would you assume you know all the answers before getting to know the new culture, environment and the people in it?

Beware of Arrogance – The Hidden Killer

John Borling, a retired Major General in the Air Force with a distinguished career that spanned 37 years, told me that what's worrisome to him is the arrogance that comes with success.

> *"It's a virulent virus. It can take you down in one unthoughtful assignation. It can take you down in one speech. It can take you down in one assignment of resources based on personal gain. It can take you down in so many ways.*
>
> *There is only one cure for arrogance – to be so scared or so hidebound by rules and regulations that you don't do anything."*

The other cure is reminiscent of the Thanksgiving prayer. That's when you go around the table at Thanksgiving and share with everyone what you're thankful for. John shared with me how one year he said, *"Dear God, I am thankful that no one found out."*

Besides having to explain what he meant to his wife, he also went on to tell me how, like smallpox, just a little bit of arrogance won't kill you, but you are sure to remember the pain. *"You almost have to fail on that, to succeed on that,"* Borling says.

The Continuum

In course of facilitating a workshop, we usually ask the attendees to pick one attribute of leaders and managers they admire most and the one they admire the least. About 90% of the time, the pair of responses is the same. **Humility** is the most admired and **arrogance** is the least admired attribute.

We have a tendency to tolerate arrogance as long as the person displaying it is very, very good at what they do. But as soon as their numbers decline – such as profits, share price, market share, employee turnover, wins/losses, home runs, points scored, etc. – it's as if all of their supporters take one step away from them. That leader or manager's behaviors are no longer accepted and he or she is suddenly left all alone, without a team to support him or her. It's not long after that the person is no longer in the job or in the organization.

In a world of Twitter, 24/7 news, and Facebook we find that ego gets attention and arrogance makes headlines. But are these winning formulae when we consider that modesty usually gets results and it's humility that makes a difference? The implications are that each of us, as leaders or managers, face the following questions: Are we confident enough to stay humble? Do we have the courage to admit we don't have all the answers?

There's a continuum between humility and arrogance that looks this. Where do you fall on it?

Arrogance...	Humility...
Burns bridges.	Builds bridges.
Makes enemies of friends.	Makes friends of rivals.
Slams doors.	Opens doors.
Is a sign of weakness.	Is a sign of strength.
Is a sign of fear.	Is a sign of courage.
Believes he/she is the only one with good ideas.	Believes a good idea can come from anyone and anywhere
Brings sorrow.	Brings happiness.
Over promises and under delivers.	Under promises and over delivers.
Destroys you.	Makes you a better person.
Talks more than listens.	Listens more than talks.
Is autocratic.	Is collaborative and consultative.
Comes in with the answer.	Asks others "what do you think?"
Can't be improved upon.	Asks others "what can I do better?"

A Story

There's a story in *The Three Laws of Performance: Rewriting the Future of Your Organization and Your Life* by Steve Zaffron that helps illustrate the points made here and throughout this book.

> *An old Cherokee chief is teaching his grandson about life:*
>
> *"A fight is going on inside me," he said to the boy. "It is a terrible fight and it is between two wolves.*
>
> *One is evil—he is arrogance, anger, envy, sorrow, regret, greed, self-pity, guilt, resentment, inferiority, lies, false pride, superiority, self-doubt, and ego.*
>
> *The other is good—he is humility, joy, peace, love, hope, serenity, kindness, benevolence, empathy, generosity, truth, compassion, and faith.*
>
> *This same fight is going on inside you—and inside every other person, too."*
>
> *The grandson thought about it for a minute and then asked his grandfather, "Which wolf will win?"*
>
> *The old chief simply replied, "The one you feed."*

A Tip of the Hat to Stephen Covey

In Stephen Covey's 1990 national bestselling book *The 7 Habits of Highly Successful People*, Habit #4 is "seek first to understand, then be understood." This is very much like the blind spot featured in this Chapter of "not coming in with the answer."

Gail Golden, MBA, Ph.D., who is the founder of Gail Golden Consulting in Chicago, shared with me the following story that I've found makes this potential blind spot more memorable.

Gail, a white, female executive coach was meeting for the first time with a new client, who was a male, African-American. There was also a significant difference in their ages. Acknowledging their obvious differences in gender, race, and age, Gail asked her new client: "*Do you have any concerns that I might not understand you?*"

Gail's client responded: "*No, I'm not worried you won't understand me. I am very concerned that you will think you do understand me.*"

Wow!

Four Words Every Leader or Manager Must Learn to Say

The enlightened leaders we interviewed for this book are not afraid to admit that they don't know it all and they ask others around them for their opinions. They have learned to say the four words that unlock insights and perspectives, as well as fostering trust and mutual respect:

"What do you think?

Contrast this with the leader or manager who comes strolling into every meeting with a tone that they're the boss and a visionary and because of that, they'll never ask for input. Instead, they tell others what they should do and think.

Which one is more likely to be seen as an enjoyable person to work for and viewed with respect?

An Over the Top Example

While working in the family office of SC Johnson, I was given the assignment of being the eyes and ears of Sam Johnson in an investment in a pencil company he had made as part of participating in a private equity fund. He and several other investors in the fund were on the board of this company, but Sam couldn't visit it as often as he'd like, so he asked me to represent him there from time to time.

After having made several trips to the company, Sam asked me to join him on a call with two other board members. His rationale was I had more firsthand experience with the operations than they did and there were several issues they thought I could help them with. They asked me *"What do you think?"* That alone was flattering, but when they made their decisions based on my observations and experience, I was in a bit of shock.

I was shocked because of who the board members were that had sought out my opinion. They were:

- Sam Johnson, Chairman of SC Johnson & Son, one of the largest privately-held companies in the US, that manufacture and market globally products that include Windex, Pledge, and Ziploc Bags.

- John Smale, former CEO of Proctor & Gamble, one of the largest consumer package goods companies in the world.

- Roger Smith, former Chairman and CEO of General Motors, the largest of the US automakers.

It was a great example of leaders demonstrating humility and empowering the people who worked for them. This experience also confirmed for me the value in speaking truth to power, which has since become one of my "winning formulas." I am respectful, but less awed, jealous, or intimidated by people of great wealth or power, than many people I meet. Being able to tell people what they need to hear rather than what they want to hear is a hallmark of a great advisor or coach.

Not Knowing the Answer Actually Frightens People

All knowledge can be broken down into three categories.

- What we know we know.
- What we know we don't know.
- What we don't know we don't know.

Think about calculus for a moment. You either know it or don't and you know which camp you're in.

By definition it's not possible to quantify the third category, but it's the largest by far. And then there's a fourth category that we've seen some leaders stray into. And it's the most dangerous of all of them. It's the category of "we don't know what we don't know, but *think* we know it." Some of us prefer to bluff our way through requests and situations, hoping not to be discovered. Why? We fear learning what the answer actually is because we're afraid that they won't like it or it will showcase a shortcoming of ours to our employees, customers or board of directors. Or, maybe we don't feel like we deserve to be in the position to which we've been appointed.

Not having answers makes some leaders and managers feel uncomfortable, even threatened, so they opt for hubris rather than humility. They tend to seek out people whose opinions most mirror their own, and as Paul Simon sang in The Boxer, "a man hears what he wants to hear and disregards the rest." As David Brooks wrote in his 2011 book *The Social Animal,* "People overestimate their ability to understand why they are making certain decisions. They make up stories to explain their own actions even when they have no clue about what is happening inside."

During our conversations with consulting clients at Leading With Courage Academy, we've seen occasions where some leaders don't want to know the answer and don't want data to support their position.

During one consulting assignment, a founding member of the organization that hired us asked that we remove a question from a customer loyalty survey we would be conducting.

The question had three parts

- *How many other companies are you using?*

- *Where does our client rank relative to the other companies you are using?*

- *If our client is not Number 1, what compels you to prefer the other company(s) to our client?*

The co-founder feared that in asking a customer, *"How many other companies are you using,"* it would open up a can of worms. He felt that this question would cause customers to say, *"Come to think of it, I should really shop this around for multiple bids. Excellent point."*

In reality, we have found that one-third of clients' use multiple service providers and have probably already had this thought. Asking such a question can show confidence in one's products and services and how the company welcomes the opportunity to convey its competitive differences and advantages. Plus, the responses would have allowed the organization to advertise how few of its customers found it necessary to use multiple companies to meet their needs as validated by an independent third party.

Despite the co-founder admitting to not having any data or research to support his request, he preferred to base his position on his many years of experience in the profession and his familiarity with the firm's clients. We acquiesced and took the question out of the survey because the integrity of the project wasn't compromised. However, the benefits of knowing the answers to this question were lost, with the firm's partners, staff, and clients being the casualties of the co-founder's hubris.

Another example is how one of the biggest, most common areas of conflict and confusion with a client of a professional services firm can be regarding their bills – as in being surprised by them and their amounts. And our research also shows that about one-third of clients are surprised by their bills, while partners believe it's fewer five percent of their clients feel this way. To avoid this tension and conflict, all that needs to be done is inform the client of the situation in advance of billing, ask then if their bills make sense, if they have a question on anything, etc.

It's relatively straightforward, common sense for everyone to be on the same page as a way to ensure a relationship is not rocky. Yet the questions don't get asked out of fear of what will be heard, with a write-off or a write-down of the bill being preferred to tackling the issues head-on.

From an internal perspective, it's easy for a newly-appointed leader or manager to come into the organization from their past successes and say, *"I know why all your problems exist."* This is the same as your doctor writing out a prescription before examining you or asking anything about your symptoms! Not always a good idea to make such assumptions, right?

Four Behaviors That Need To Be Visible To Others

Whether internally with employees or externally with customers, clients and vendors, here are some key traits that a leader or manager has to put on display as often as possible:

Leaders Listen

If you are to lead others, you need to have your finger on the pulse of what makes the people tick and keep an open mind. A new leader or manager coming in from the outside can't walk in and assume they know everything.

So, take ample time to understand the landscape you're about to lead by asking others and listening before even thinking of recommending anything. That includes knowing about the problems that have existed before, the positive traits the company has, what the culture is like and more.

Stephen Sadove, then chairman and leader or manager of Saks, Inc., said the following in a New York Times interview a few years ago:

> *"I always tell people new to my organization when they come in, I want you, in your first three or four weeks, to jot down every time you have an idea or a question about how things are done and then stick it in your drawer. Just whatever it is...why are they doing it this way?*
>
> *I don't care whether it's good or bad; I don't want you to even talk to anyone about it. Just write it down and stick it in the drawer. And at the end of three or four weeks, I want you to look at the sheet. Maybe you'll say: 'Now, I understand that.*

Now it makes a little bit of sense to me.' Or you may look at it and say, 'That still doesn't make any sense to me.'

Then I want you to sit with me and we're going to talk about them. Invariably, I find some really good ideas that make you say: 'Why are we doing it this way? It makes no sense at all.' I've seen little things, big things, waste in the system and a lot of duplication of work. Things like that come out of it."

Get buy-in and support

Listening gradually builds a sense of trust and communicates that you are going to incorporate what you've learned from feedback into your next steps as a leader. So, when you're finally ready to show some of those next steps, convey the link between what people told you and why you're doing what you're doing going forward. This provides a greater likelihood of them buying into what you're "selling." Don't just do what you want to do - it doesn't work well to unilaterally cram what you've learned on your own elsewhere down your employees' throats.

Educate and upsell customers, clients, and employees by asking questions

You're more likely to become a trusted resource and advisor, both internally and externally, by the questions you ask rather than showing off your expertise and credentials.

Asking questions of customers about your products and services can enlighten them on your entire range of offerings. When you assume they know all of that (which they usually don't), you'll miss out on additional revenue. Just because you have it on your website doesn't mean it's anywhere near top-of-mind with your customers and clients.

So, as you ask for and listen to their thoughts, consider a natural bridge to a *"Did you know we also offer..."* statement that points them toward something additional your company brings to the table. I can't tell you how many times we've seen customers do this and then say, *"They said they never knew we did that!"*

Strike a balance between legitimate privacy and appropriate transparency

I remember an occasion when the leader of an organization that was being merged into another, larger organization didn't want to share with the employees some facts about changes in their benefits and incentive compensation plans. His argument was the news would be a distraction from getting the deal closed, plus they'll never know about the changes until after the transaction has been finalized.

I cautioned against this strategy, arguing that he should have the courage to act as if the employees would find out, which they always seem to do, and that their reaction would be much worse than being direct and honest about the changes. It's a lesson learned from the Watergate and Arthur Anderson/Enron scandals– the cover-up is worse than the crime.

Being honest, direct, and transparent usually turns a difficult situation into one that is manageable. It's one thing to be guilty of doing something wrong, but it's an entirely different matter to deceive people and hide the truth from them. You can usually earn forgiveness for the former, while the latter is much less forgivable. It's made worse by how you may never be able to win back the trust of the employees.

Driving In Heavy Traffic

The onboarding of a new leader or manager is a lot like merging into heavy traffic during rush hour at 5 pm on a Friday. All the other drivers are focused on getting to their destination as quickly as possible, so you need to be careful. You use the on-ramp to accelerate and be at the same speed as the traffic you're entering. When you want to change lanes, you need to first look in all directions and then execute your maneuver without slowing down. *When you want to change direction, you need to signal your intention to others and then position yourself in the correct lane.*

Six Key Questions

When a leader or manager enters a new role, the clock is already ticking, and a lot of eyes are on him or her to make an impact. People are watching and listening carefully to you. They're picking up on cues in ways they weren't sensitive to when you didn't have your new title. So, you need to have a disciplined, structured process for understanding what's happening, especially within your organization. Three areas that are crucial to quickly understand are:

We regularly help newly appointed executives identify the business risks and quality of these areas using three assessments, one specific to each of them. This process has the benefit of quickly bringing to the surface the misperceptions and misalignments that require attention and clarification. It also builds consensus and the sense of urgency necessary for addressing the challenges.

At the end of the process, we regularly hear how the leadership team has a much better understanding of the business and that they haven't had such a focused conversation since they started it

As part of this process, we ask six key questions that we originally learned from Big Swift Kick, a sales strategy and sales force improvement company:

1. **What's the future look like?** When we're having breakfast three years from now and you're knocking it out of the park, what will you be telling me about?
2. **How are you doing on those things today?**
3. **What obstacles in your way are stopping you getting from here to there?**
4. **What have you tried already tried to fix the situation?**
5. **What's been the impact on your company?** I don't suppose it has cost it any money? Or had any impact on you personally?

The sixth question we always ask before moving from one question to the next is the one we shared in Chapter 1. That simple, easily overlooked, two-word question is *"**Anything else?**"* We like it because it ensures we've mined the questions for all of their insights.

Three Exercises to **Build Your Courage Muscles**

➢ **Meet with three people who have been with your company for one to three months.** Ask them to share with you their observations and questions about how or why things are being done the way they are. Two ground-rules: 1) don't try to take over the conversations and 2) don't dismiss anything each person tells you.

➢ **In each of your meetings over the coming week, vow to ask to one or more participants** *"what do you think?"*

➢ **Schedule a meeting with each of your five best customers and clients over the next two months.** Ask them how your company is doing and what else you could be doing improve your relationship with them. Don't forget to ask them one of our favorite questions, *"anything else?"*

Take Aways to **Be Leading With Courage**

➢ Hubris – excessive pride or self-confidence – is a career killer. Sometimes it grows out of previous experience. Sometimes it is the byproduct of fear and insecurity. Whatever the cause, a blind spot to be on the alert for is confirmation bias -- searching for or interpreting information in a way that confirms your pre-conception of something.

➢ Regardless of what prompts it, when a newly appointed leader or manager or board member feels it's necessary to play the role of the all-knowing, all-decisive great and powerful Wizard of Oz, then his or her behaviors can be damaging and demotivating.

➢ A much better role to play is one that channels the curiosity of Magellan, the ability to motivate others of John Wooden and the humbleness of Warren Buffet. It involves asking others what they think, being a good listener, not fearing what you'll hear and keeping an open mind.

➢ Avoid the temptation of coming in with a "recipe card" approach to solving an organization's problems. Doing so is the kiss of death.

Notes

Chapter 4

Focus on Fewer and Bigger

"If you chase two rabbits, both will escape."
Anonymous

Most of the leader or managers and board members we interviewed told us how they heard these types of comments upon starting in their new roles:

- *"We're doing too many things."*
- *"We're drowning in routine tasks."*
- *"We're trying to be all things to all people."*
- *"We're stretched too thin."*
- *"We've become too complex."*

A funny thing happens when organizations add people, product lines, brands and locations: The tasks, details, exceptions and surprises that need to be managed seem to increase at an even faster pace. The resources required to manage these complexities – time, people, and money – are limited and usually seem to be shrinking.

The challenge for most companies is that revenues and profits increase linearly, while complexity grows exponentially. All of this leads directly to **the third blind spot that leaders and managers need to be on the lookout for – attempting to do too much.**

Growth Won't Solve All of Your Problems

Growth always seems to be top-of-mind for management. It could come from a variety of avenues. It could be organic. It could come from mergers and acquisitions. It could be as the result of new products or new services. And in all its various forms, it's usually accompanied by an obsession with growing faster than the competition.

While it seems that a lot of the challenges you encounter will go away if you can just grow faster, that's probably not the answer to everything. In fact, many times, growing faster actually creates *more problems*!

Let's do a quick self-check of your business at this very moment. At Leading With Courage Academy, we've found successful business have at least the following:

- Processes, systems and controls in place that will sustain the business
- A well-defined, written plan
- Stable, committed management team
- Diverse customer base

What if any of these aspects are missing and you double your growth rate? The company could be in trouble. The stage may be set for the business to expand rapidly, but without a team to manage it or the processes to deal with the new challenges, how long can that growth be sustained? What's the quality of that growth and how profitable will it be?

In such a scenario, your problems aren't being solved by growth – they're actually being made worse. Even if you receive more business from an existing client or industry. Growth has the power of revealing and amplifying serious flaws in your organization. A typical lesson that's learned is that more of everything isn't necessarily better and, when you do get it, it rarely meets your expectations.

We aren't naïve and advocating you shouldn't be growing, of course. Growth is critical to the long-term success of a business and to you as a leader of that business. So, what can you do help achieve your vision? One thing that is mission critical is to keep the number of objectives, goals, strategies and measures small. It comes down to one word – **focus.** This idea also applies to the number of people in the organization, the number of locations and SKUs, how many vendors you use and just about every aspect of the business.

Four Benefits of Focus

Reducing the number of initiatives will allow you and your organization to:

1. ***Move faster* because it will be easier for individuals and teams to communicate and make decisions.** With fewer options to compare, contrast, analyze, debate and defend, more time will be spent doing and less time deciding.

2. ***Learn more* because focusing a few things leads to deeper, real insights than when multiple projects are being pursued at the same time.** The faster you can drill down to the core issues, the sooner you'll discover the insights needed to get you on the path to success.

3. ***Accomplish more* thanks to moving faster and learning more.** It's often said that the best way of getting nothing done is to try to get everything done at once. Focus accelerates the rate at which you learn – especially from failures, both yours and those of others – which sets you up to accomplish more than organizations that aren't concentrating on fewer things.

4. ***Create value* by accomplishing more than your competitors.** Creating value, in turn, makes it easier to attract and retain the talent you need to achieve your vision. It also makes it easier to get funding from banks, negotiate strategic alliances and differentiate your company from others in the market.

The Six Attributes of Focused Companies

To focus on fewer, bigger ideas and initiatives, your approach to managing the needs of your group, department or organization has to take on the following characteristics:

1. ***A driving belief* – growth and success will come from having fewer, stronger arrows in your quiver.** Rather than shooting more arrows at more targets – as in more services, more industries, more niches, more customers, more countries – with the hope of scoring more bull's eyes, you'll be making larger commitments to fewer, bigger targets to reap larger rewards.

2. *Value drivers* – **growth and value creation will come from a vision that's easier to understand and communicate, an organization with fewer layers and levels and simpler processes.** Instead of working to extend and expand all of your brands and services, you'll focus your resources on a few of them – a few products or services, a few industries, a few markets, etc.

3. *Complexity* – **instead of accepting the incremental costs and inefficiencies of complexity as unavoidable, the focused organization treats complexity as the enemy.** The company is instead driven by the beauty, economics and challenge of keeping things simple.

4. *Leadership* – **in a focused company, the leaders act as facilitators who remove the obstacles to progress.** They're about gaining buy-in, securing funding, agreeing on timing, etc. – and helping their teams discover the answers. Contrast this with the organization whose leaders act as if they are visionaries and provide all the solutions.

5. *Resources* – **in organizations with many initiatives and priorities, budgets constrain what can be accomplished.** In focused organizations, the constraints are imagination and curiosity. At the same time, they don't have bottomless sources of funding and must be fiscally responsible.

6. *Planning and processes* – **focused organizations prefer to plan quickly and then stick with those plans for the long term – such as three years.** They don't make sudden changes in their strategies. They live with the consequences of their decisions. The conventional company spends more time planning, but then has a tendency to get distracted or impatient when it comes to executing their plans and fails to implement them. Conventional companies are also quick to shift to a new strategy when the current one isn't delivering the intended results. The focused

organization is concerned about action and getting it right, while the conventional company is more focused on analysis, reporting and formal meetings.

Key to Success – Doing Your Homework

Because you'll be focused on fewer initiatives, you have to make better, more informed choices about what those initiatives will be compared to conventional organizations. Since your commitments will be more significant and you're making them for the long term, you need to do your homework before locking them in.

We've already discussed some of that homework in Chapters 2 and 3 – understanding your organization's culture and an honest, detailed assessment of its health. With so much riding on these insights, you need to be sure you know what should be changed and what you have to accept. Moving forward without first seeking feedback from your key stakeholders is setting yourself and the organization up for failure.

It's a common problem. KPMG, for example, found that 78% of the directors and C-level executives attending its Fall Roundtable Series during November/December 2015 were "very concerned" or "somewhat concerned" that management tends to use "more of the same" assumptions – regarding key factors and uncertainties – in setting strategy.

Let me give you an example: At Leading With Courage Academy, we're regularly asked to propose on assessing the loyalty of clients to the professional services firms they're using. This involves face-to-face interviews and/or an electronic survey of a sample of the firm's clients. These projects take about three months to complete and the payback is typically about 500:1 – for each dollar invested, we usually identify $500 of incremental revenue opportunities in existing clients that the firm was not aware of.

To realize the additional revenue, all firms have to do is arrange a conversation with their clients and partners having good, but not even great, skill at closing on sales calls.

Sounds like a no-brainer, right?

Well, we've occasionally been told that the managing partner has decided he or she doesn't want to risk "bothering their clients." Instead, he'll just ask his partners what they think their clients need.

That's an excellent idea in theory, but in reality, it's misguided. Our surveys show that ***in about 50% of partner-client relationships, there is at least one significant gap in a partner's perceptions of that client*** *and in about 10% of the relationships, there are five or more gaps.*

These gaps are on key attributes of the client experience, including the likelihood to refer the firm to others, what compels a client to prefer another firm, whether the firm is capable of meeting the client's needs for the next 2-4 years and how much effort it takes on the part of the client to get a response to a request.

Partners should be asked what they think their clients need, but their feedback should not be treated as an accurate gauge of the unmet and emerging needs of the clients they serve. Why? Because many of them don't know what they don't know, but think they know it.

Here's an extreme example of this disconnect: Our firm was engaged to conduct a client loyalty assessment for a mid-size law firm. 49% of the clients surveyed were classified as being "loyal" to the firm based on their responses to four of the questions in the assessment. This is lower than we what usually see, but not alarming. We then asked the partners serving those clients the same four questions, asking them how they thought their clients responded.

Based on previous assessments we've done, we expected the partners' scores to be 5-10 percentage points less than the clients – somewhere between 40% and 45%. This is because partners in professional services firms tend to be under-raters of the value they add to their clients.

However, even we were surprised by the partners' perceptions: ***They thought that just 1% of their clients were loyal to the firm!***

The implication was they were leaving millions of dollars on the table (which we had quantified too, and the managing partner agreed with) because of their low self-perception of the value they were adding to their clients. For example, they weren't asking for referrals. They were afraid to bill for out-of-scope work. They weren't charging enough for their services. All of these were things that they agreed they were not doing.

Despite experiences like those described above, many managing partners prefer to develop their strategic plans, make critical staffing decisions and commit resources to create new products and services using unreliable insights and perspectives.

Maybe this helps explain the commoditization of their services and the consolidation that's taking place in their industries. This may be what's prompting most managing partners of CPA firms to ask: "Who should we merge *with* or merge *in*?" and "What do we need to be doing to stay relevant?"

The point of these examples is that doing your homework is a prudent step that pays dividends. It usually doesn't take long or cost much. In addition, when you don't have the resources within your organization to do it, you can outsource the task. So, the question is, why *wouldn't* you want to do your homework?

Execution

Strategic choices make a difference only when they're executed. Neither hope nor good intentions are strategies for moving the needle. When you're focused on fewer initiatives, execution excellence needs to be one of your organization's core competencies.

Among its best attributes are:

- Making decisions and holding meetings closer to the front lines, where the action is.

- Eliminating distractions and complexity by streamlining, reducing and cutting wherever possible – this includes unnecessary meetings, shelf keeping units (skus), packaging variants, layers in the organization, and unprofitable customers.

- Revisiting processes to see which are no longer required, especially those that are obsolete, but to which the organization is emotionally attached. Some examples of these are:

  - Issuing live paychecks rather than directly depositing the payments into employees' checking accounts

  - Mailing paper invoices to customers instead of sending them PDFs electronically

  - Having customers send their payments to you through the mail rather than to a lockbox or accepting ACH transfers

- Stopping things that don't generate a return, such as reports that aren't being read or used.

- Sharing best practices across departments, locations and subsidiaries.

- Communicating your successes and learning from your failures.

Another facet of focusing on fewer and bigger initiatives is to be disciplined when making your choices. Let me explain. Not all customers in a niche or market are the same. While they may seem to be a good fit in terms of annual revenues, geographic scope, reputation in their industry and need for your solution, their mindsets can be radically different and not compatible with what's best for your company.

How One Company Makes Choices

Todd Brook, CEO of Envisionit, has developed a structured and disciplined process for scoring how well prospects and current customers fit with his company's strengths, values and frame of mind. He and his team then choose whom to work with based on where they are today, how much opportunity there is for improvement and the impact they can have on that business.

Using a calibration guide to help ensure a level playing field and consistent application of the ratings, Envisionit scores the mindset of prospects and customers on a scale from 1 to 12 on the following areas:

- Focus on immediate growth
- Collaborative and appreciative
- Transparent, open, and honest
- Bureaucracy free
- Passionate about the business
- Willingness to experiment
- Confidence and commitment to a direction
- Track record of success

This chapter advocates for focusing on fewer, bigger initiatives. The next chapter is directly related to this concept – managing multiple activities at the same time.

Three Exercises to **Build Your Courage Muscles**

➤ **What are your organization's key initiatives for the next 12 months?** If there are more than five on your list, which can you eliminate or postpone?

➤ **Identify a monthly or quarterly report that takes a lot of time to prepare, was a favorite of your predecessor** (even better if **he or she designed it) and one that you don't find helpful.** Stop issuing it and see who notices.

➤ **Ask your direct reports about their priorities for the next year.** Which of them are they most excited about? Which of them do they have concerns about? In both cases, why?

Take Aways to **Be Leading With Courage**

➢ No organization, large or small, can effectively manage more than five strategic initiatives without losing focus and decreasing the likelihood any of them will be implemented.

➢ Have principles for making your decisions and share the rationale for the choices you make with those impacted by them.

➢ Initiatives and priorities must be easy to understand and clearly communicated to all of the company's stakeholders. Not just one time. Among companies that claim to have a strategic plan, 95% of the employees don't understand it (David Norton and Robert Kaplan, Harvard Business Review, October 2005). As Yogi Berra said: *"If you don't know where you're going, you'll end up somewhere else."*

➢ The metrics used to track progress against your initiatives must be shared broadly.

➢ To focus on fewer, bigger initiatives, people must be held accountable for meeting their commitments, to the best of their abilities, without reminders. This doesn't only apply to your organization's leaders, but to everyone who works for the company – employees, suppliers, consultants, etc.

Notes

Notes

Chapter 5

Delegate, Automate, Do, or Eliminate

"No person will make a great business who wants to do it all himself or get all the credit."
Andrew Carnegie

Quick – name the biggest threat to your business. While you're at it, name a couple more. Make a Top 10 if you like.

Now here's a surprise for you: *None* of those threats will be as big and scary as the moment a leader or manager says these five words: ***"I can do that myself."***

That sounds fair enough on paper. Yet, before long, time passes and that leader or manager hasn't been able to move the initiative much farther at all. While the leader or manager's full *intention* is there, the initiative never seems to get his or her full *attention*. What accounts for that?

A common culprit that prevents this is related to the blind spot discussed in Chapter 4 – attempting to do too much. In this chapter, we'll explore that blind spot's first cousin – **when a leader or manager tries to do it all himself.**

Where It Begins

The commitment to undertake the project may have started off all wrong to begin with, as he or she didn't have the humility to understand that outsourcing the project was the right move. Suddenly, in believing they can do everything, that leader or manager has just done a lot more harm than good in the way of addressing some critical initiatives for the company's progress.

How can you prevent this from happening in your environment? It begins by understanding the symptoms of this inertia.

I've heard *"I can do that myself"* enough times from a leader or manager by now that my response has typically been: *"Well, you can do it yourself. But do you have the time, interest and expertise to do it? Do you have a process for tackling the project in a structured and disciplined way? What will you stop doing in order to get things done 100%?"*

If you're in this type of position, you may feel a degree of guilt in delegating or outsourcing a project, thinking, *"I should really be the one doing this. If I delegate the project or hire a consultant, why do they need me?"*

This isn't strictly a leader or manager issue all the time, either. We routinely see it up, down, and across organizations.

For example, Marketing people don't always have the strategic voice in the direction of the company that they'd like or should have. However, if they had a tool at their disposal like a client loyalty assessment, they'd indeed have the keys to the kingdom. They'd be the ones driving a lot of processes because they'd possess so much data on clients, strengths, vulnerabilities and more. They'd have a genuine seat at the table so to speak and their stock would go way up from a strategic value perspective.

To get there, they may very well need some help from an outsider. Yet, because they wouldn't be the ones conducting the process, some marketing directors feel threatened and kill the initiative.

So, let me help you take a good hard look in the mirror in a different way: You say you're supposed to be doing certain things rather than outsourcing those tasks. But be honest with yourself – why aren't you checking off all the boxes on your list in a timely fashion? Just because you say you should do something doesn't make it real and a priority.

When you delegate or outsource a task or project, it becomes real. At that point, multi-tasking is happening and you're getting more done.

Delegate, Automate, or Do

Here are seven questions you should be asking about the tasks on your "to do list" to help you decide which ones you should be delegating, automating, or doing yourself.

1. Does this task move the business forward? If not, why is it even on your list? If it must be done, then move to Question #2.
2. Is this a recurring task?
3. Can you automate this task?

4. Does the task require your judgment each time?
5. Is there time to delegate this task?
6. Does anyone else have the skills to do the task?
7. Can you train someone else to do the task?

What you have here is a decision tree to help you manage your task list. If the decision is to "delegate" the task, then you'll be facing another choice – to whom should the task be assigned?

Delegating to the Wrong Person

We were working with Jill, a leader in a mid-size packaging materials company, who told us how she struggled to delegate more tasks to her staff and team members. Jill said it was because the results she got back usually disappoint her. Her justifications for putting in long hours and doing so much of the work herself were:

- It's too complicated to explain tasks to them.
- It takes too much time for me to train someone.
- I'm going to spend too much time fixing their mistakes.
- I find that it's faster and easier to do it myself.

The issue wasn't one of lacking a team to whom Jill could delegate tasks. There were about 20 people in her group, including a few who had just finished college and a couple who had been hired with significant experience from other companies. Jill was happy to tell us how none them had performance issues, so her challenge with delegating tasks wasn't due to having a team of "duds."

After a few more minutes of probing, it was clear Jill's challenge was due to how she regularly delegated tasks to the wrong people. Her blind spot was not matching the task and her style of supervision to the person's competence and interest in the task being assigned. By treating everyone and all tasks the same way, Jill's disappointment with the results she got should have been expected.

To help Jill make better choices of who to delegate tasks to, we provided her with the following decision-making model. We also paired with it with some simple tips for overseeing the tasks. Here's the three-step delegation model we shared with Jill:

Step 1

Answer two questions about each candidate, rating them on a three-point scale of 0, 1, or 2.

1. How competent in the task is the person being considered for the assignment? (0=not competent to 2=very competent)
2. How interested in the task is the person being considered for the assignment? (0=not interested to 2=very interested)

Step 2

Add together the two ratings in Step 1

Step 3

Interpret the total score and manager the project as follows:

0 = Find someone else to do the job

1 = Tell the person exactly what to do and supervise him or other as it's being done

2 = Create a detailed plan with the person and have him or execute it

3 = Have him or her create a detailed plan and review it with them before they start

4 = Give the person an end goal and tell them to ask you for help if they need it

This model led to an immediate improvement of the quality of the results, more tasks being delegated by Jill, and a better trained group. It also increased the engagement of team members and a reduction in the number of hours Jill was putting in.

Since then, we've suggested to clients that they also use this model on themselves to decide which tasks they should be doing and which ones they should delegate.

Roadblocks to Progress

Those five scary words, *"I can do that myself,"* are often accompanied by five convenient excuses many leaders and managers make that create self-imposed roadblocks from moving forward. These traveling companions are:

1
"We don't have the time to do it this year."

When we speak to companies about onboarding a newly appointed leader or manager or conducting a client loyalty assessment, we're really talking to them about increasing revenue or improving profitability. So, when we hear, *"We don't have the time to do it this year,"* here's what's really being said:

> ➤ *"We don't have the time to generate incremental revenue."*

> ➤ *"We don't have the time to understand where we're most vulnerable to the advances of our competitors or to save or strengthen relationships with our customers."*

> ➤ *"We don't have the time to ensure that we don't make the same painful mistakes that we've made before."*

Leaders and managers should be engaging in these initiatives and they may very well want to. But they get torn in so many different directions by being in positions of authority that they don't have the time. And it frequently begins from the very moment a newly appointed leader or manager steps into the role.

In fact, it's not just making time but that it's going to take them longer because they don't have a process or little experience dealing with the problem at hand.

Sam Zietz, CEO of TouchSuite shared with me his view on delegating tasks to others. He believes that *"80% of somebody else is far better than 100% from (him) because (he) can have 100 people at 80% and that's scalable."*

Sam went on to tell me about his philosophy of inviting someone to be a part of Touchsuite's management committee. *"You have to be better than me at whatever it is your area is. If I'm better than you at it, then you're not ready. Why? Because I want to be surrounded by people who are better than me at those areas."*

For example, his Chief Operations Officer needs to be better at operations than Sam, his Chief Financial Officer needs to better with numbers, his head of R&D needs to be better at product development and his Chief Marketing Officer needs to be better at marketing than Sam.

Sam's philosophy on delegating and being surrounded by smart people is just one of the reasons that Touchsuite has been repeatedly been on Inc. Magazine's "Inc. 5000" list of the fastest growing private companies in America. It was also named one of the "best entrepreneurial companies in America" in 2018 by Entrepreneur magazine's Entrepreneur 360 list.

This is also where a qualified consultant can be most helpful. It's not going to be their first rodeo and you get to take advantage of their cumulative experience, benefitting from all the mistakes they and their clients have made, as well as all the refinements they've stumbled upon and insights they've gained.

2
"I know what's worked elsewhere and I can do it again here."

Each of the leaders I spoke to for this book had one experience in common – they had worked in another company, most in a different industry, before being appointed CEO. This breadth of experience, an ability to see things from different perspectives and how this makes a person more well-rounded and agile, seems to be one of the keys to success in these demanding roles. But it comes with a dark side that the executives I interviewed were very much aware of and avoided.

It's nice to think that there's a plug-and-play method of solving problems from one company to another. It's seldom the case, however. A strategy that worked well for one organization will rarely deliver similar results when it's applied unchanged in another. It's just not that easy. If it were, leaders and managers wouldn't be paid as much as they are.

There are always going to be differences in the situations, both obvious and subtle – culture, personnel, goals, budgets and so forth.

➢ What worked for Pepsi didn't work at Apple – all you need to do is ask its former CEO, John Sculley.

➢ What worked for Google didn't work for Yahoo – just ask its former CEO, Marissa Mayer.

➢ What worked for Apple and Target didn't work at J.C. Penney – ask its former CEO, Ronald Johnson.

3
"Our information is just too sensitive to trust to anyone else."

Really? Do you defend yourself in court? Or do you go out and get the best attorney you can afford? Same goes for designing advertising campaigns and preparing tax returns.

I'd say most people would choose using an experienced expert because they know they shouldn't be trying to navigate something that important on their own. So why wouldn't you apply the same thinking to your business? Keeping it in-house doesn't guarantee it gets addressed in a timely manner nor does it guarantee that it's going to be done better.

Whether it's onboarding a newly appointed leader or manager, assessing customer loyalty, managing a logistics network or developing breakthrough software applications, one thing holds true: *If that isn't what you're good at, why are you doing it?*

Give it to people who are passionate about it because that's all they do and they have an exceptional track record. If you're in a leadership role, you're not detracting from your own position by involving others who can complement your strengths with their own. The outside experts aren't a threat. Using them will make you look even better.

4
"This is definitely important…
we just can't do it during busy season."

That's the wrong way to look at it. While it may be busy season for YOU, it's usually not for your customer.

Companies that are inward looking to such an extent shouldn't be surprised when their perceptions of their customers are not aligned with those customers' perceptions of themselves. Understanding the customer's view of your company and the service they are experiencing is important every minute of every season. And by the time your "busy season" has passed, it's not unusual to hear the next Self-Imposed Roadblock.

5
"We'll do it next year."

Sounds like a commitment, but the problem is that next year never comes. Ever. This is the quintessential line from someone who doesn't see it as a priority now, tomorrow or years in the future. No matter how adamant they are that they'll attack it at the first chance they get…someday.

It always reminds me of a scene from the W.C. Fields movie *Mrs. Wiggs of the Cabbage Patch*, in which an unmarried, older woman played by ZaSu Pitts suggests that she and W.C. Fields *"...should get together sometime soon."* To which he replies, *"let's just say sometime."*

The deeper issue that usually gets in the way of making progress is **fear.**

- **Fear of looking bad or not looking good** in front of colleagues or a board

- **Fear of change** because change is uncomfortable, usually involves conflict and isn't a billable activity.

- **Fear of hearing things that aren't positive** or not aligned with your perceptions of a situation

How do you get over these fears? Come up with ways to reduce the risks that are holding you back.

For example:

- **When you're worried that the work won't get done right or on time, set up a follow-up system for each task that you give to others.** In the beginning, take the time to sit down with the person to whom you're assigning the task to make sure he or she understands the deliverables and your expectations.

- **When you're stressed out about what you might hear from customers or clients, start with a small sample.** This will allow you to get comfortable with the idea, refine the process and prepare yourself and others for what you are likely to hear when you seek feedback on a broader basis.

When you're holding back on implementing a change initiative, build support for it by first talking to opinion setters. Share the initiative with those most likely to be against it. Rather than lobbying them for their support, learn why they oppose it so you can prepare for their dissent and perhaps even modify the plan to reduce their concerns.

Three Exercises to **Build Your Courage Muscles**

➢ **Take this self-test of your delegation skills:**

- Do you keep getting busier and busier?
- Do you tend toward perfectionism?
- Do you neglect to elicit the opinions of others or accept their ideas?
- Do you often feel it's just easier to do it yourself?
- Do you believe it's up to you to solve all of your company's problems?
- Do you find it difficult to switch off from work and that this is disrupting your relationships at home?

If you answered "yes" to any of these questions, you might need to improve your delegation skills.

➢ **Identify tasks to delegate or eliminate.** Make a list of all the things you do each day, week, and month. Then take a piece of paper and divide it into four quadrants, (*see next page*) and put each task into one of them

After placing each task into the appropriate quadrant, look at the tasks in the bottom half of the chart. If you or your organization does not have the time or resources to do all of them, which of them can be eliminated altogether?

Then ask yourself which of the tasks that remain in the lower half of the chart can you delegate to others? Especially those tasks in the lower right quadrant?

Like

Unique Ability	Like Doing It
Love Doing It	Good At It
Great At It	Gives You Enjoyment
Gives You Energy	
Don't Like Doing It	Do Not Like Doing It
Good At It	Not Good At It
Does Not Give You Satisfaction	Leaves You Feeling Frustrated

Don't Like

> ➤ **Use the three-step delegation model to decide to whom to delegate the task to and your approach to supervising him or her.**

Take Aways to **Be Leading With Courage**

➤ In your effort to prove to yourself and the company that you are the right choice for the position, you may feel you need to do everything yourself.

➤ When you attempt to handle multiple complex challenges at the same time, you run the risk of looking foolish, burning out and/or failing.

➤ Your end in mind should be to go from managing all of the details of a project to *directing* all of the details by managing only a few of them.

➤ When you master this skill, there's no limit on how much you can grow your business.

➤ You'll also find you enjoy the job more, help your employees expand and develop their skills and able to allocate more of your time to the initiatives that benefit most from your involvement.

Notes

Notes

Chapter 6

Foster Trust and Alignment

"A leader takes people where they want to go. A great leader takes people where they don't necessarily want to go, but ought to be."
Napoleon Bonaparte

When a leader or manager of an organization is appointed or comes into a department, he or she will be under the microscope.

Adrienne Stevens is the former CEO of Notions Marketing Corporation based in Grand Rapids, Michigan, a global distributor of arts and crafts supplies that picks, packs and ships over 30,000 packages a day. When she arrived at the company from the aerospace industry, it didn't take long for Adrienne to realize that everything about her was being watched – including what kind of car she drove, what time she came to work, whom she interacted with and more. Employees were making judgments and forming opinions of Adrienne without even knowing her.

Being aware of this, she made it a point to be visible in the organization from the very start. She would get to know people, communicating with them clearly and frequently. Before long, it was apparent to all within the company that Adrienne was the kind of leader who was fully accessible and transparent in terms of her goals and expectations.

When asked about alignment, most of the leaders interviewed for this book responded along these lines: Alignment is achieved when a leader creates a sense of urgency around, builds consensus for and gains commitment to a vision or plan. They also spoke about how alignment describes the quality and strength of a company's culture and the relationships that exist between and among employees, teams, leadership and the organization itself.

Based on personal experience, alignment doesn't happen by accident. It must be coaxed and nurtured. Because it has so many dimensions and facets, it's not easy to create and it's a challenge to maintain. For these reasons, it should not be taken for granted. **Failure to build alignment or not building it fast enough is another blind spot newly appointed leaders and managers need to avoid, minimize or recover from.**

Communication is the Key

Communication is the key to building alignment. It is communication that is:

- Direct, accurate, candid and jargon-free
- Transparent
- Consistent
- Balanced between being too much and too little, good news and bad news
- Two-way
- Using channels that are appropriate to the audience and the message being delivered

Patrick O'Brien, the former CEO and now vice chairman of Paris Presents, Inc., a branded beauty products company in northern Illinois, shared with me how he proactively created alignment with the private equity firm (PE) that owned the company. Before accepting the offer to be the CEO, Patrick set up a half-day meeting with the directors of the PE firm to understand a wide range of matters including:

- How they liked to work and how Patrick liked to work
- What each of them is like at their best and worst
- How each individual deals with direct and honest conversations
- Their respective plans and preferences for creating shareholder value
- How often they wanted to meet and their preferred methods of communication
- How each of them would behave when results are 95% of the plan

Share the Bad News Too

Proactively sharing the bad news is one of the hallmarks of alignment and transparency. When information is withheld, the vacuum that is created is usually filled by people second-guessing each other and assuming the worst. This leads to them being unproductive as they spread false rumors that always seem to amplify the feelings of anxiety already present in the organization. By only sharing the good news, people will feel you are misleading or manipulating them and your credibility suffers.

Our company, Leading With Courage Academy, regularly works with organizations whose leaders are quick to share the news about winning a new piece of business. But when they lose a customer, that never seems to get mentioned. It's as if they believe that if no one knows about it, then the customer didn't move their business to a competitor.

Without any insights into why the customer left and nothing being shared across the company regarding these reasons, the impact of the loss is further compounded. In the end, this hurts the company and diminishes the credibility of those leaders as people become cynical about the successes that are celebrated.

Selling the Furniture to Make A Point

Aaron Gillum told me about the time he was Managing Partner of Caerus Investment Partners and leading a turnaround at a client that was dangerously close to running out of cash.

The company had exhausted its credit lines, the investors weren't willing to contribute more capital and the banks were nervous. At an all-employee meeting, he told the group about the dire situation and how all of their jobs were at risk if the situation wasn't addressed quickly. He then shared some specific, simple actions each of them could take to help turn things around.

An employee raised her hand and asked Aaron *"just how bad is it?"*

Aaron proceeded to tell her how he had just seen the FedEx driver in the lobby of the office. After signing for the day's packages, the driver commented on how much he liked the sofa in the lobby, telling Aaron that he had visited the company many times and each time he noticed that sofa.

In no time, Aaron not only sold the sofa in the lobby to that FedEx driver, but he also helped him load it onto his truck in return for his personal check for $600. As soon as the sofa was driven off the property,

Aaron was eyeing other non-essential office furniture as a source of cash. That's how bad things were.

Bang! Urgency and commitment were generated among all of the employees, but more importantly, so was trust. By being direct and honest, Aaron didn't provoke alarm. Nor did he distract everyone from staying focused on the bigger objective.

Four Exercises to **Build Your Courage Muscles**

➤ **"See how the sausage is made."** You might've heard this phrase that's used to describe what it means to view the work of real people in the trenches of your business. The popular show *"Undercover Boss"* typifies what happens when leaders or managers get a true understanding of the challenges their employees experience every day. Come down from the ivory tower and see what it's like to work on the manufacturing line of your business or go on sales calls if you're a professional services organization.

➤ **Prepare an organization chart that includes pictures of each employee on it.** Make it your mission to recognize every single employee. That way, when you see them in person, you can call them by name. It's a simple act that goes such a long way to convey how much you care about building relationships.

➤ **Make sure all perspectives are heard before you make a decision.** There's a difference between alignment and agreement. People in organizations aren't always going to agree, but they need to align as a team. When you hear all perspectives before making a decision, it's then reasonable to expect everyone on the team to align with that direction. Not to mention you'll severely decrease the likelihood that there needs to be any meetings after the meeting or a covert opt-out of the decision that's been made.

➤ **Have each person on your team take an Everything DiSC® assessment and then run comparison reports between you and each of them.** *(This was discussed in Chapter One. Please go to page 16 to revisit comparison reports.)*

Take Aways to **Be Leading With Courage**

➤ Great alignment demands constant nurturing from a leader who builds consensus. Not everybody needs to agree, but they do need to align.

➤ Communication in the name of alignment can't be all "good news" all the time. Leaders need to remember to share the bad news for transparency's sake too.

➤ Expressing urgency and gaining commitment is key among employees but not without building trust through an honest and direct approach.

➤ Assume that when you ascend to a leadership role or enter the organization as its new leader, all eyes will be on you – everything about what you do and say are undergoing intense scrutiny from employees. Meet that environment head-on by ensuring you are accessible for answering questions and clarifying agendas.

Notes

Notes

Chapter 7

Identify Your High Performing Team – Part I

The People Who Will Subvert Your Efforts – Underperformers, Termites, and Covert Change Killers

Protecting under-performers always backfires. The worst thing, though, is how protecting people who don't perform, hurts the people themselves.

Jack Welch
Former Chairman and CEO of General Electric

When you come into a leadership role at a company, you can't help but hear what employees say about this person or that person:

- *"Watch out for Karen - she has a bad attitude."*
- *"Marty has a strong work ethic."*
- *"Jason's performance is terrible, and he should've been fired years ago."*

Let's not pretend that such chatter doesn't permeate the atmosphere at times.

While you need to keep an open mind about people, ideas and alternatives, you also have to avoid **one of the most common blind spots of newly appointed leaders – holding onto underperforming team members too long.** I don't think there was an executive interviewed for this book that didn't mention this as something they've been guilty of and wished for a "do-over."

Kyle Seymour, President of S&C Electric, pointed out something that nearly all the CEOs I spoke to also mentioned: *"If you work on the people issues first, everything else gets easier after that. If you have the right people in the right places, they end up doing a lot of your work for you, making it easier and faster to get to your goal."*

So how do you honestly evaluate which people are going to be your best assets and which ones are going to be problems?

First, it's important to remember that not everyone is as they seem.

One person can be an obvious pink slip candidate for their consistent lack of performance – an **Underperformer**.

Another person clearly hates any form of change and is a lover of the status quo. They slowly but surely eat at momentum from the inside, which makes them a **Termite**.

Someone else can be all smiles and well-liked but secretly be saying things against you behind your back – a person I refer to as a **Covert Change Killer**.

Secondly, you have to allow people an opportunity to show what they can do – not just for your evaluation purposes today but also for what they could become tomorrow. When you do, special circumstances may arise in which a seemingly difficult person to work with, when used properly, could actually be a great asset for the company.

Let's take a closer look at each of these Underperformers, Termites and Covert Change Killers so you know what you're dealing with faster.

The Underperformer

Can I tell you something about the very first person I hired? It's a person I regret hiring -- a classic Underperformer. Although, in my defense, it wasn't entirely my fault he was hired.

Let me take you back to that time. It was the first opportunity I had as a supervisor to hire someone. We'd interviewed several people and I'd found an outstanding candidate. She completely fit the bill for what I was looking for and I couldn't have been more excited to bring her aboard.

Then there was another candidate we'll call George who had all the right skills in his background, but we just didn't click in the interview. It didn't feel right and I didn't want to hire him. Conversely, I was confident the candidate I preferred could get a lot of work done rather than create more work for me as her manager.

Done deal, right?

"We like George. Sorry, but you have to hire him," my two managers told me.

Needless to say, I wasn't thrilled.

Still, I knew if I hired "their guy" and he didn't work out, George would be easier to get rid of because my managers could admit they were wrong. If I'd hired someone they didn't want, I'd hear "*I told you so*" until the end of time.

I tried to be optimistic about George, but he didn't give me much reason for it before long. One misstep after another came and we weren't advancing the initiatives we wanted to as quickly because of George. I was working harder because of him too. If George were a car in a dealership lot, he'd be the clunker you could never get rid of.

It took a solid six months of George continually screwing up for us to remove him. But it didn't take me six months to know George was a dud and an Underperformer. The sooner you can spot an Underperformer, the better because dislodging him or her may not happen overnight. This is especially true if you're working outside the United States where it usually much more difficult and expensive to terminate an employee. The adage "hire slowly, fire quickly" always seems to be good advice.

Sometimes the cause of being an Underperformer is that as a company grows, a once valued and rewarded set of skills becomes an obstacle to achieving future success. This is particularly true when that growth is due to a customer base that is becoming larger, more complex and more demanding than before.

Brian Grady, CEO of Gorilla Group, an innovative e-commerce solution provider in Chicago, found this to be the case. As their customers shifted to being larger and multi-faceted, their needs became more complex and the buying decisions took longer and involved more people. To solve the problems of this evolving customer base, a different set of the talent and skills was needed compared to that at the inception of the company.

This is quite common. The skills and talent needed to grow a company from zero to $1 million are very different from those required to grow an enterprise from $1 million to $10 million, $10 million to $100 million, $100 million to $1 billion, etc. To go on this ride with you, a person needs to have the capacity to learn and develop.

Brian and his team had to make some tough choices regarding staffing if they were going to refocus the company on what the market would be demanding 2-3 years in the future. This wasn't easy given that some of their people had been employees from the beginning and the market for labor was tight and competitive. But these, along with some other strategic choices, would prove to be critical choices. Gorilla has seen its projects go from a low of $35,000 to a high of $2,000,000. It now has about 350 employees compared to the 10 when Brian bought the company and Gorilla's revenues have grown 71% over the past three years.

When the people can't or won't adapt to the new needs, then it's up to you to make some courageous choices. These choices are made more complicated if the people impacted are the same ones you leaned on to help you start and build the business – family and friends. Most of the CEOs I talked to who started their businesses from scratch told me stories about this. Without exception, it was one of the most stressful, emotional and difficult decisions for them. It never got easier, but they said they waited too long to make it.

When I asked Sam Zietz of TouchSuite what finally prompted him to make these tough, but necessary decisions, he told me it was when he began to resent these people being in the organization. He resented that they were holding the team and company back from achieving their full potential. He knew it wasn't their fault – it was his – and he was self-aware enough to take the blame and to be transparent, fair and respectful when he told them they were parting ways.

Sam has found that when he's made these very difficult decisions early on, the people end up thanking him, leave the company on good terms, refer business to TouchSuite and speak highly of the organization. When he's waited too long, he has found those people leave the company with a lot of bad feelings, are more likely to post something negative on the Internet and may talk poorly about him behind his back.

Every CEO I interviewed had gone through this sort of experience and their solutions were always the same – make the tough choice, do it sooner and be respectful of the people impacted the most by it. *This experience is one they vividly remember and never want to repeat.*

Cutting Compensation Seldom Solves The Problem

Dan Formeller, Senior Chairman of Tressler LLP, an eight-office law firm headquartered in Chicago, has learned that reducing an under-performing professional's compensation only results in a lower paid, under-performing professional.

The under-performance feeds the rationale for under-compensating, which further feeds the rationale for further under-performance because the professional says *"if that's all you're paying me, then that's all you're going to get."* Management, in turn, says, *"if that's all you're going to give us, then this is all you're going to get."*

It's a downward spiral that almost always leads to the conversation you should have had months or a year earlier about how this is not working out.

How One Leader Handles These Conversations

Here's an example of how Todd Brook at Envisionit has started some of these very, very difficult conversations.

(Employee enters Todd's office)

Employee: *Hi, how's it going?*

Todd: *Not good at all. Grab a seat.*

(Employee is visibility shaken.)

Todd: *I didn't sleep a minute last night. And what sucks is, as bad as I feel, you're about to feel worse.*

I'm letting you go today.

I want to explain to you why and walk you through that.

We're at a point right now where I need to restructure. I need to make sure that we've got the right capability at the right time to take us to the next level.

You've been incredible, but if I don't restructure, I risk hurting the rest of the business for the wrong reasons.

(Employee is given time to process what he's just heard.)

Todd: *Take your time, you know the routine because you've had to let employees go as well. We've got to escort you out, but before we go any further, I want to protect you as an individual.*

I want us to align on how you want us to approach this. I believe in transparency and honesty and we both know I can just say that we let you go today. I could say something else. What would you like me to say?

What is noteworthy about the start of this conversation is that it's short and Todd gets to the point immediately. He's also got someone else in the room with him to make sure nothing is missed or misunderstood and can serve as a witness in case the employee claims you said things you did not. Todd is respectful of the person's privacy and the contributions he's made to the company. In the end, you should be telling people this sort of news in the same way you'd want to hear it.

Four Questions to Ask When Making Tough Decisions

I learned about these four questions while working for Helen Johnson-Leipold, the eldest daughter of the fifth generation of the family that owns SC Johnson. I needed to make a tough decision that challenged the principles underlying the organization and asked Helen what she would do. She didn't answer my question directly, but shared with me some advice her father, Samuel C. Johnson Jr., had shared with her.

The four questions Sam shared with Helen and that Helen shared with me immediately struck me as a form of the Hippocratic Oath that's sworn to by physicians to guide and inform their medical practice. In this case, those four questions are:

1. ***Is it the "right thing" to do for the person impacted?*** It's not about treating everyone the same. It's about fairness, which is different and more important than equality.

2. ***Is it the "right thing" to do for my organization?*** If your decision were to appear on the front page of the New York Times, would you be proud to stand by it? If not, that may be an indication of the decision to make.

3. ***Is it the "right thing" to do for the communities we serve?*** Many leaders think that if a decision is made in the best interest of their company, then it's the "right" answer. But they neglect to ask if it's in the best interest of the community, which can get them into trouble.

4. ***Does it "feel right" to me?*** This can be the toughest of the four questions because it requires you to put aside your biases and preferences aside.

When you answer "yes" to **each** of these four questions, you're likely to be making decisions with greater consistency and confidence. (When you answer "no" to each of them, it's probably a "fall on your sword" type of issue.) But it's not enough to just make the decision. You then need to tell those affected by it why you're making it.

Since then, the internal voice in my head has asked these four questions whenever I'm faced with difficult choices including:

- Should I terminate an underperforming employee or client?
- Should we hire a family member or friend?
- Should we stop investing in a "pet" project?
- Should we award a bid to a customer?
- Should we discontinue supporting one of the organization's charities?

The Termite

> Lee's former boss: *"We can't fire Fred. He's the only one who knows how to get information out of the system."*

> Lee: *"I can get someone to replace Fred in a week."*

Ah, good ol' Fred. The guy who'd been with the company for 25 years. Fred bled the company's values and was a cheerleader all the way. Everybody liked him and he knew how to get data out of the company's systems better than anyone else.

So why on Earth would we want to get rid of him?

A funny thing about Fred: Once you got to know him, you realized he was so stuck in the past, it was ridiculous. He loved the company we used to be and possibly even who we were today. But if you wanted to talk to him about the future? Forget it. Any talk of change and Fred would just shut down. It became like pulling teeth to get this historian of the Good Old Days at the company to do anything new. The situation becomes even worse in your environment when a person like Fred also happens to be a rainmaker.

Fred never really wanted to push the envelope. He was what I would call satisfied with satisfaction. We're talking about the quintessential "*If it ain't broke, don't fix it*" character.

I'm sure you've come across enough Freds in your career – the person who talks about how they've always "done it a certain way" or is quick to point out that the idea you have today was already tried three years ago. The individual who tells you how to build a clock when you ask him what time it is. Fred was the original "Director of We Tried That" in the organization below.

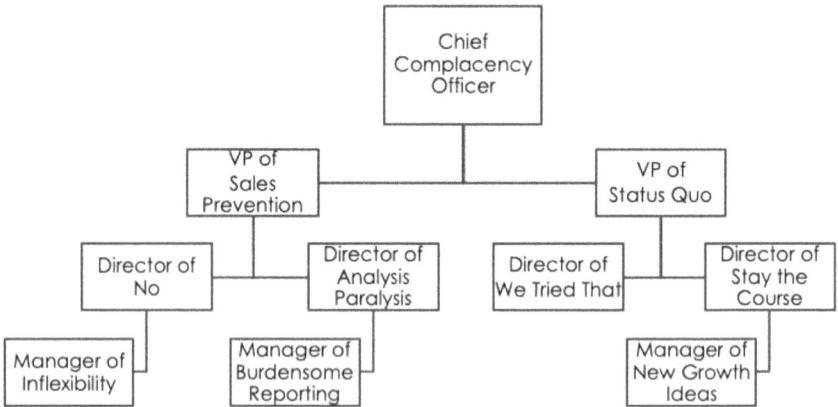

Fred also wasn't a big fan of anyone trying to make a change in his own department. He was quick to point out how much of an expert he was in a particular area of the company and that nobody had a right to poke their nose into his business.

You have to watch out for the Fred in your company because a person like this is what I refer to as a Termite – the longer you keep him around, the more damage he does. It's likely he'll eat away at the momentum you're trying to build. Termites are a giant drain of time and energy who can do great harm.

It wasn't hard to build a compelling case for showing Fred the exit: At the end of the day, key initiatives weren't getting done due to his constant resistance and we weren't dealing with the trends and threats in our industry. We were falling behind.

If you have termites in your home, are you going to ignore them and pretend they'll go away on their own? No. Then don't keep around a Termite like Fred for nostalgia's sake. He'll just eventually play a part in bringing the house down.

The Covert Change Killer

How fast can you spot a Covert Change Killer?

One week. Sometimes even less than that.

That's right. You can spot one just that quickly. Because as covert as they act, the Covert Change Killers have dead giveaways in their actions and body language too.

The Covert Change Killer passes you in the hallway, cracks a giant smile and seems like the brightest ray of sunshine in the place. They'll tell you how if they were ever stranded on deserted island, you're the one person they'd want with them. Then, when you close your office door, they'll be talking to their cubicle and office mates about how they doubt you'll last six months. They're dangerous because not only are they skeptical of buying into your plan, but they're also secretly attempting to spread that skepticism to others and poison their minds against you.

Covert Change Killers also tend to be arrogant, profoundly political, and very good at what they do. It's the latter trait that fuels their arrogance and ability to gain the attention of and hold the respect of their superiors. These all combine to give the illusion that they care and are the solution, not the problem. The issue is they only care about themselves, their personal agendas, and maintaining a grip on their power. For them it all comes down to greed, power, and self-interest.

For example, as soon as I met a new direct report who arrived for our first meeting without a pad of paper or a pen, I said to myself, *"now here's a Covert Change Killer."* At first, it might have seemed that she was just disorganized. But it became clear during our meeting that she just didn't care enough to retain anything I said or she felt she couldn't learn something from me. Sure enough, she would prove to be trouble for both me and the rest of the team members who had to deal with her.

The source of the Covert Change Killer's resistance is typically one or more of the following:

- They thought they should have gotten your job

- They thought their best friend who applied for your job should have gotten it

- They're afraid you'll expose their insecurity and vulnerabilities

- They see you as a threat to their power and influence

- You're smarter than they are

- People like you more than them

- You've displaced them as one of the organization's "shiny new objects" or star performers

How Do You Spot An Underperformer, Termite or Covert Change Killer Faster?

You'll know a blind spot when you see one or more of the following tell-tale signs:

1. **They're not open to change and are very happy with the status quo.** Even though they can and have failed enough times, the actual problem with people who are Underperformers, Termites and Covert Change Killers is less about skills than you expect. Dig deeper and you'll find that the real issue is they don't want to change. They want to keep everything the way it is at the status quo.

2. **They don't play well with others.** They tend to be sole contributors and are not used to working in a team, so they take down the overall performance of the group. They may have been pushed into a higher-level role and think they have all the traits to succeed as a leader when they don't. They're scared because deep down, they know they don't have what it's going to take to do the job.

3. **If they manage other people, they tend to have higher turnover rates than their peers.** They are usually micro-managers who are quick to blame others on their team for the problems they've created. Nothing is ever quite good enough for them, but they're passive-aggressive and won't tell you that to your face. I've found they like to manage through fear, with a command and control style. They're also among the very best at playing office politics.

4. **They hate being under the microscope.** They've usually received consistently excellent reviews from multiple supervisors. But were those reviews as honest or in-depth as they could be? Probably not.

   Consequently, they've believed their own "press clippings" for so long that it's almost impossible for them to change. They'll tell you how "good enough is good enough" and that your expectations or standards are too high.

5. **They may be a key asset who thinks you cannot survive without them.** They may be a famous person in your industry, a technical guru, a rainmaker or the owner's son or daughter. But if they're regularly held up as an example of what's not tolerated in your culture, are frequently seen violating your company's values and/or behave as if they're made of Teflon, then you should be asking yourself these questions:

    - What's the best and worst that would happen if they were no longer in your organization?
    - How would you fill the (short-term) gap that's created?

Unfortunately, be forewarned that this may put you in the position of being the "bad guy" as the first person to ever tell them what they genuinely need to improve upon. Don't be surprised if you get pushback from this critique and hear responses like, *"I've been here 20 years and nobody ever gave me a bad review. This is the first time."* They have no interest in being self-aware. They think they're perfect and you're the one with the problem because nobody else has ever had an issue with them before. Or so it would seem.

Lloyd Carney, when he was CEO of Brocade Communications, a data and storage networking firm that's now a subsidiary of Broadcom, shared this story with Adam Bryant that was published in the New York Times in August 2016. I think it's one of best at making the point that everyone is replaceable.

> *He (Lloyd's uncle) used to say all the time that everybody is replaceable. He used to do this thing called a bucket test. He would be arguing with one of his employees, and he'd call me in and say, "Get a bucket of water." So I'd bring the bucket of water to the room, and he'd say, "Lloydie, put your hand in the*

water." Then I'd take it out, and he'd say to his employee, "See that hole that Lloyd left in the water? That's the hole you're going to leave when you leave here."

The guy was usually trying to get some big salary, trying to explain how invaluable and important he was. Once every eight months or so, my grandfather would call for the bucket of water. So I have a pretty high bar for calling someone irreplaceable. If I hear that, I'll say, "Why? Is it Steve Jobs? Is it Einstein?" Everybody's replaceable.

6. **They don't have the skills to succeed now.** Oh, they once did. But because they're change-averse, they didn't evolve their skill set. They're still using old technology. And they have no interest in learning anything new either.

7. **They don't want to do what they're asked.** Who said this is a democracy? When you're asked to do something by your boss, you generally should do it whether you like it or not, right? Yet these individuals will dig in their heels, question why they have to do it and maybe give you some attitude to boot. You don't need a "yes" man or woman, but you don't need someone to be difficult all the time either.

8. **They take up _way_ too much of your time and energy to manage.** They may be competent but when it comes to interacting with others, they're an outright disaster. They suck all the energy out of the room, partially because they are masters at playing the victim and blaming others for the problems they've created. If it's so terrible of an environment for them and they don't want to change, it's probably best to set them free.

Of course, there are a couple of other types of individuals who could very much be on your side. We'll take a closer look at them in our next chapter. Be forewarned – they won't leap out at you as clear allies in your mission of change. But once identified and managed properly, they could prove as powerful as anyone in helping you get to where you want to go.

An Example of Making Tough People Decisions

Craig Duchossois, Chairman & CEO of The Duchossois Group, Inc., shared with me a lesson he learned about not sticking with under-performers too long. He had recently gone through enormous change in one of his companies where, in the five years prior they had enjoyed success and Craig, by his own admission, became too cocky. He allowed a sense of complacency to take hold because the numbers were always going in the right direction. Yet, he came to realize that even when the numbers go in the right direction, you sometimes find comfort when you shouldn't. In this case, he learned that organizations can outgrow their executives and that that it's very difficult to deal with someone who "brought you to the dance" to say, *"It's time for you to sit down and let someone else be on the dance floor."*

Craig knew that among the responsibilities a CEO is to have lines of communication vertically throughout the organization. Reflecting back over the years, he remembered having had to make three changes in over 40 years because the organization, customers or suppliers came back and said *"Were you aware of...?"* After validating the feedback from enough credible and trusted resources, he moved quickly to make the appropriate changes. In two instances, he gave two CEOs 12 months to get their acts together, but for whatever reason they didn't believe him. They thought that Craig was more interested in annual earnings than creating long-term value appreciation. He made the tough, courageous decisions to let them go. According to Craig, the two CEOs were competent and very good in many ways, but they had a short-term orientation. And that's not why they were hired.

Accountability and Compassion

During my conversation with Ed Wehmer, President & CEO of Wintrust Financial Corporation, we talked about what happens when an employee isn't working out. Here were Ed's thoughts on that:

> "We have an obligation to those people. I tell our guys, *'If you hired this guy, and he's not working, that's your problem. You made the mistake. Either you didn't help him, or you hired wrong. You are accountable and responsible*

> *for that, so you should be working with the person. What's the plan?'*

If he doesn't work, cut him. It's all part of the accountability. Take the blame.

You've really got to be in touch with every level of the organization. You've got to make sure all your people are heard because often those are people dealing with the customers every day. If you don't listen to them, well, they're the ones who are hearing it or seeing something. They've got good ideas. You've got to be able to make sure those ideas are being filtered up."

Just Remember -- The Fish Don't Eat the Macaroni

It's not likely that your Underperformers, Termites, and Covert Change Killers will suddenly meet your performance expectations, embrace change or stop undermining you and your plans. If your diagnosis is correct, then the cure is usually to have the courage to get involved and go outside your comfort zone.

I learned this lesson at an early age – 13 years old, to be exact. I was on a weeklong camping trip in the Superior National Forest in northeastern Minnesota with 15 other boys my age. The area is a pristine wilderness and it's essential that it be preserved. Among the ways this has been done is requiring campers to "pack out" their garbage.

Earlier in the day, we had been fishing and had had a lot of luck catching small mouth bass and panfish. Along with the freshly caught fish, we had macaroni and cheese for dinner. And there were some leftovers. Our counselors told us to go far from the campsites and bury the uneaten mac and cheese and then wash out the pots in the lake. It seemed like a reasonable request, except for the fact it was getting dark in the woods and that's no fun for a 13-year-old to venture out into.

Remembering how the fish were biting that afternoon, one of us had the great idea of not going into the dark, scary woods as we had been told. Instead, we would wash out the pots in the lake and the fish and loons would eat the macaroni that we hadn't finished while we slept. Who would ever know?

Being thirteen, this sounded like a darn good plan to us, so that's what we did.

The next morning, our counselors got us up at about 6:00 am. It was earlier than usual and it wasn't because we had a long day's journey ahead of us. They had discovered the shortcut we had taken the night before and informed us how we wouldn't have time to eat breakfast. That was because we'd be picking up the hundreds of pieces of slippery macaroni the fish hadn't feasted on overnight that were now littering the lakeshore.

We spent the next few hours in mid-calf deep, ice-cold water gathering up bits of pasta that we then buried deep in the woods. I've not looked at a box of macaroni and cheese the same way since that summer day nearly 40 years ago.

The moral of the story: Don't expect your problems to take care of themselves. The fish don't eat the macaroni and it's not likely that your Underperformers, Termites, and Covert Change Killers will be suddenly be transformed into highly productive and valued members of your team without you intervening.

Three Exercises to **Build Your Courage Muscles**

➢ **Make a list of the problems that you're not addressing that you're hoping will take of themselves.** It might be an employee matter, a good customer who is very hard on your staff, an unprofitable product that consumers love or declining cash flow.

> Knowing this:
> – What are you going to do about them?
> – When will you do it?
> – What does success look like?

➢ **Do you have any Underperformers, Termites or Covert Change Killers in your organization?** If not, what makes you so sure of your answer?

➢ **Add a calibration meeting to your next performance review cycle.** This is a meeting where you and your direct reports talk about each person that reports to them and agree on their performance rating for the past year. Everyone comes prepared to discuss how he or she plans to rate their employees and explain the reasons behind the ratings. When done correctly, the values and strategic objectives of the organization will help frame discussions. The result is that ratings are consistently applied across the company.

Take Aways to **Be Leading With Courage**

➢ Sticking with Underperformers, Termites, and Covert Change Killers too long creates internal dysfunction that erodes your credibility, undermines your authority and ultimately subverts your success.

➢ You want to *think* that everyone is on the same page as you. But you are probably wrong. It's worse than that. Nobody that works for you is willing to tell you the exact and total truth. You need to be observant, a good listener and trust your gut.

➢ Be fair and objective. When John Borling first comes into an organization as its leader, he always says this to the people he's working with: *"I want to and I hope to earn your loyalty. I must give you mine."* But he doesn't say for how long and then he begins to carefully assess the organization.

➢ While it's no fun telling someone that you've outgrown them or that they're holding back the rest of the organization, tolerating poor performance and bad behaviors creates damage throughout the organization. Just as you can see only 10% of an iceberg, so it is that the impact of Underperformers, Termites and Covert Change Killers is much broader and deeper than you're aware of. It affects you, your employees, customers, vendors and service providers.

➢ When you come into a new role, you need to ask yourself the following questions about the team you've inherited:
   – Is my team capable today of doing what we need to be done?
   – What training do they require?
   – Is it within their DNA to ever get there?
   – Does time allow me to get them there?
   – Do I need to hire someone from the outside who already possesses these skills or expertise?

Notes

Chapter 8

Identify Your High Performing Team – Part II

The Good Guys – Disruptors and Chameleons

"Here's to the crazy ones. The misfits. The rebels. The troublemakers. The round pegs in the square holes. The ones who see things differently. They're not fond of rules. And they have no respect for the status quo. You can quote them, disagree with them, glorify or vilify them. About the only thing you can't do is ignore them. Because they change things. They push the human race forward.
While some may see them as the crazy ones, we see genius. Because the people who are crazy enough to think they can change the world are the ones who do."
Steve Jobs, 1997
Apple, Inc.

We've talked about the cancers of a culture who are the most likely to push against your initiatives as you roll them out – the Underperformers, Termites and Covert Change Killers. On the other hand, there are a couple of other types of people who could rally to your side – they just may not be apparent allies at first, so let's examine their characteristics.

The Disruptor

What do you call someone who may seem difficult to work with...but at the same time could become a terrific asset when used in the right situation? Think about it. What if some people happen to be trapped in the wrong department for their skills? What would it mean if they had a different set of people to interact with them?

You might be dealing with a **Disruptor.** Let me give you a perfect example of one.

In one of the stops along the way in my career, I was asked to assume a Controller-type role at a company. My boss was to be someone I'd worked with in the past who was highly visible in the organization. Thanks to that relationship and the good track record I'd had, it looked like a terrific fit.

That is, until I learned about one of the other people I'd be closely managing.

This individual was a fellow we'll call Rick. Rick wasn't just a person you'd describe as "a handful." He was a *career-limiting nightmare* in every sense. You didn't know what was going to come out Rick's mouth next, when he was going to say it and how. The immaturity level of Rick was off the charts.

However, if I wanted to take this job, I had to work with Rick. There was no getting around it. What horrors would be in store for me?

As it turned out, Rick was probably the *best person* to have inherited. Why? He was so out-of-the-box for what his responsibility called for. He got bored with routine concepts and tasks, bristling at them. Consequently, Rick also had fabulous ideas. We did some of our very best work as a team when Rick was around because he could challenge our team to take our ideas up a notch.

Rick wasn't a pain after all. What he was, in actuality, was a Disruptor.

Again, at first glance, Disruptors may not seem like they fit in. In several ways, they don't. Rick rubbed people the wrong way all the time. Yet, in the right role in the right department working with the right people, Disruptors thrive.

It's easy to mistake the Ricks of the world as Covert Change Killers or Termites. But when they shake things up in a positive way, those may be people whose instincts are good for the purpose of pushing the envelope. This may call for them to be encouraged and nurtured rather than feared and despised.

So, they don't "go with the flow" like everybody else. Is that automatically bad?

Not necessarily if the situation is right. Mind you, there were times when Rick never knew when to stop trying to challenge his co-workers, so he could come off as abrasive. But that's also when a Disrupter needs to be controlled and managed.

How do you manage a Disruptor?

I've made it a habit not to look at performance reviews, particularly when starting any new relationship, because I don't want such reviews to color my opinion of someone. Instead, I recommend **having a sit down meeting that's candid.**

When I first started working with Rick, I wasn't afraid to be brutally honest to his face in a sit-down meeting. It sounded like this:

> *"Look, Rick. You're really giving people some issues. They're saying certain things about you that I have to share because, frankly, it's not just one person saying it. So, I want to help us figure out how you can better work with them. I can't afford you continuing to do what myself and others have seen you do. I also want to know – how are you and I going to work together? I want to talk about my personal concerns with you and how both of us can work to make our boss successful."*

However, you can't solely drive the agenda. Rather, it's just the opposite. Give this a try – every week or every other week, you set a meeting with the Disruptor. But tell them that **you want <u>them</u> to bring the agenda to the meeting.**

Suddenly, that reversal of agenda setting totally changes not only the dynamic but also the person's "buy-in" as well. It becomes their meeting and that's a good thing. Guide them with questions if you like such as:

- *What do you want to tell me about?*
- *What's going on in our department and what should I know about?*
- *What happened this week that you're proud of?*
- *What didn't go as well as you would've liked?*
- *Where do you need my help?*

When I asked them to bring the agenda, 95% or more of the people I asked brought such a list. All I was trying to do was stay aware of what was going on in the organization because, after all, I was getting those questions from supervisors above me.

Here's another topic that should be added to the list above that Pam Lenehan, author of *"My Mother, My Mentor: What Grown Children of Working Mothers Want You to Know"* (Archway Publishing, 2015), shared with me. Pam had a weekly meeting with the CEO of the company to whom she reported – we'll call him Mike. Because both Pam and Mike were crazy busy, their paths didn't cross often enough and the weekly meetings were their way of staying aligned on priorities, informed of progress on critical projects and in agreement on the essential tasks for the coming week. Mike also asked that Pam come to each of these weekly meetings prepared to tell him something that would make him smarter.

Talk about a win-win. I can't think of a Disruptor I've known who wouldn't find this an engaging challenge.

The Disruptor is far more likely to embrace a structure that encourages their input. The Termite or Covert Change Killer? That's a much different story because they see this as micromanaging or bullying.

The Chameleon

The Chameleon is a person who can change and blend into the background of their environment seamlessly, even if it's a new one – in this case, a different title and role. Everybody around this person makes a much bigger deal about the transition because, on the surface, they can't believe that someone from another part of the company or different background could possibly succeed in a new position. They're quick to judge – too quickly, in fact – because The Chameleon has the versatility they never expected. All they needed was a chance to show they could thrive.

I witnessed a good instance of a Chameleon benefitting the company as he was replacing a Termite.

As I was beginning a new role overseas in the Paris office of a company, I was excited to bring my fair share of ideas to the table. However, every time I had a new idea and whenever a particular project manager was in the room, I was met with, *"Well, we can't do that – it's against the law here in France."*

Not entirely knowing the culture in France just yet, I trusted this project manager's opinion. Over time, I came to learn that it had nothing to do with legalities in France. It was that he simply didn't want to change!

We were eventually able to move the person in question out of that project management role, but we nonetheless had a void as a result. Who would lead our biggest projects now?

The answer came from a very atypical place – at least at first glance – when I picked a very talented IT person for the role we'll call Muriel.

While others in the company were quick to question why I'd want an "IT geek" like Muriel for a project management position, I knew we had to look beyond titles. Experience had shown me that I.T. people could be perfect for project management roles because when implementing a software package or system update, they follow a time and budget-constrained protocol in a disciplined and structured way. Many IT people also have a good working knowledge of the bits and pieces that make up the business and are able to see the unintended consequences of changes.

By taking someone who had those skills and re-applying them to a different role, we found an even better fit than before. Muriel was detail-oriented but could see the big picture. She was process-driven and timeline-driven. As a result, during projects with timelines we could never push back, Muriel wasn't "just the I.T. geek" everybody thought she was. She was the Chameleon who changed her skin on the outside by moving to a different position, but the inherent skills made for the challenge she'd had all along. She moved us forward and made up for any lost time we'd had when the previous person was in her position.

It would be great if everyone in the company sang your praises upon your first day in a new leadership role, proclaiming that they'd follow you to the end of the Earth on any initiative.

Ah, what a beautiful fantasy.

The reality is that relationships take time to build and trust has to be earned. In addition, your best allies aren't always going to be obvious. That difficult individual could be just the Disruptor you're looking for. That talent buried in another department may be a Chameleon just asking to be plucked for your challenge.

By taking an active role in evaluating everyone from your Covert Change Killers to your Disruptors, you can more quickly – and accurately – assess which people are genuinely behind you and which ones will drag you down with them.

Three Exercises to **Build Your Courage Muscles**

➢ **Identify a Disruptor and a Chameleon in your organization.**

Then get together with each of them separately to learn more about:

- An experience they've had that they are the proudest of
- The types of environments and managers they feel bring out the best in them
- Any ideas they have for improving processes they've dealt with
- Telling you something that will make you smarter

➢ **Add a Disruptor or a Chameleon to a project team that has been struggling to make progress.**

➢ **When selecting a team for a new project that is expected to be very challenging, include a Disruptor on it.**

Take Aways to **Be Leading With Courage**

➢ A Leader With Courage keeps an open mind about people, ideas and alternatives. The person that some view as a Termite or Covert Change Killer may actually be a Disruptor.

➢ When you need some help seeing things you may not have considered, ask someone who has an idea or view that's different from yours this question: *"Why don't you tell me more about why if we do it this other way, it's going to be a mistake."* Rather than making them justify where their idea is right, taking this tact should help you see why what you're thinking might be wrong.

➢ The notion of the calibration meeting (the third exercise in the previous chapter) can help teams identify their Disruptors and Chameleons.

Notes

Chapter 9

Be Open to Innovation and Novelty

*"Status quo, you know,
that is Latin for 'the mess we're in.'"*
Ronald Reagan

Think about this: Of all the companies that belonged to the Fortune 500 in 1955, only 53 are still members of that illustrious list today.

How could this happen to so many seemingly successful companies? Was their drop off a result of a new competitor entering the market, globalization or advances in technology? Actually, not as much as you'd expect. In fact, it's often said that the biggest threat to a business comes from within its very walls – *complacency and satisfaction with the status quo.*

The Pattern of Decline

A company on the downward slope makes many of the same mistakes time after time. It's just that predictable in some instances. It's too bad that by the time leaders spot the pattern, it's much too late in the game.

The pattern of decline generally unfolds like so:

- **A company is simply "crushing it" in the market.**

- **The company's great success leads to it locking its focus on one or a few successful offerings.**

- **Now the company starts to really believe its own press clippings.** *We're the best in town! In fact, we're the* *best anywhere! Our products and services sell themselves! All our clients love us!*

- **By now, the leaders of the company are earning more than they ever imagined when they started their careers.** They never think that something even better will displace their star performer.

- **The leaders start to play it safe.** After all, life is great. Why rock the boat or fix what doesn't appear to be broken? Except that "safe" is about to take on another meaning – being far too conservative to make strong progress.

- **The situation is made more tenuous when the company fails to update its technology and change with the times**. Meanwhile, the competition is feasting on their complacency.

- **The coup de grace is delivered by focusing only on the customer of today and not anticipating the unmet and emerging needs of those customers tomorrow.**

Does that sequence of events sound familiar? It should. We've seen it in companies such as:

- **Blockbuster Video**, which failed to see mail order and live streaming as threats to its business model.

- **Xerox**, which invented the mouse, the graphical user interface and laser printing, but didn't embrace these innovations in their products. Instead they chose to sell, license and give away the technology to others.

- **Kodak** and **Polaroid**, which entirely missed the shift to digital photography.

- **Hostess**, which focused on Twinkies and Ding Dongs while consumer preferences moved on to healthier food choices.

- **The U.S. auto industry**'s lack of response to the threat posed by Japanese cars in the 1980s.

Today's "best" often becomes tomorrow's "minimum acceptable." We see it with technology and company performance. The jump to applying the analogy to individuals is not hard to make.

This brings us to a key blind spot that leaders and managers need to avoid -- **not seeing or reacting to changes in their situations and relying on old tactics that have worked in the past at other companies.**

The Pressure to Deliver Results

Most leaders and managers come into their jobs with terrific track records of success. There is an expectation that you'll be able to do for your new company or team what you've been able to do for others. That usually translates as accelerating growth, improving profitability and doing so in a relatively short period of time.

The pressure to deliver results can be so high and the tolerance for risk of failure so low, that it's understandable why some executives prefer to go with what they know worked in a prior situation rather than look for better solutions. Maybe what worked before will work again, but you need to ask yourself these questions before going with it:

- How similar are the situations? Be honest.

- Is your decision based primarily on your experience with the answer and how you prefer to "play it safe?"

- What, if any, are the unintended consequences of implementing the same solution in the new environment?

- How open have you been to considering alternatives that might lead to an even more substantial increase in long-term value for key stakeholders?

The leaders I spoke to while researching this book clearly preferred to manage opportunities rather than risks and to take accountability for their failures.

Missing the Obvious

Many of us are blind to innovation and novelty because we aren't able to see what we don't expect to see. It's not our fault, as Dr. Mahzarin Banaji points out in her book *"Blindspots: Hidden Biases of Good People"* (Delacorte Press, 2013) - that's just the way our brains are wired.

In Banaji's book, she shares a classic experiment that demonstrates this. Subjects were given a task to watch a video of people passing a basketball and to count the number of times the ball was passed from person to person. In the middle of the video, a woman carrying an umbrella walked through the scene. Afterward, when the subjects were asked if they noticed anything unusual, *less than 20% could remember seeing the woman with the umbrella at all!*

Our ability to focus on what's most important allows us to filter out distractions, take shortcuts and make faster decisions. This worked well for our ancestors when hungry wild beasts confronted them. It continues to serve us today when we go to a flea market looking for one specific treasure from among the tens of thousands of items that are for sale.

However, this ability to filter and focus comes with a terrible downside: It keeps us from seeing anything new that doesn't fit our beliefs. It keeps us from learning. This is why we believed for centuries that the Earth was flat, the sun and other planets revolved around the Earth, diseases were caused by poisonous "bad air" and the continents were stable and didn't move. Our predecessors believed these "facts" with the same certainty that we believe today that smoking causes cancer and increasing levels of greenhouse gases have led to global warming.

Vikas Bhatia, then CEO of Kalki Consulting in New York City, a company that provides IT security advice and training to small to mid-size businesses. He shared with me a story of how it's easy to become so committed to innovation and forward thinking that it can prevent you from achieving your objectives.

Vikas told me about a company he knew well that was very proud of how it automated everything. Its proposals were automated and went directly into their quotes that in turn went right into their invoices. Emails were fired off, databases were updated and meetings were added to calendars all based on pre-defined and programmed triggers.

This sounds great...until Vikas pointed out the consequences of relying on ten or more different, disparate, cloud-based technologies each talking to the other in a timely manner. If just one of them were to go down, the impact on the business could be significant. If more than one went down at the same time the business might be damaged beyond repair. When the company began thinking through those potential consequences, it slowly changed each one of those technologies. They realized they had gone too fast and too far on their approach to innovation. It's also a great example of how a strength taken to an extreme can become a weakness.

While even a blind squirrel will occasionally find an acorn, the challenge many leader or managers told me they've had to tackle is getting an organization – with its unique collection of culture, silos, divisions, teams, brands and personal agendas – to recognize when a great, threatening or game changing idea is standing right in front of them. When they do see it, what do they do with it?

Christine Robins from Char-Broil shared a terrific example of how powerful this can be. Early in her tenure as CEO, she and her team introduced a new operating norm called "Speak Up." They wanted people at all levels of the organization to know it was okay to raise their hand and speak their mind.

Right after sharing this new norm at an all-employee meeting, a forklift driver from the warehouse came up to Christine. The employee told her how he knew he wasn't supposed to approach the CEO, but in the spirit of Speak Up, he just wanted to tell her how he used their smoker products and how he had made some modifications to them because they could be a lot better.

Christine listened to his ideas and then introduced him to the head of R&D, someone he had never met despite having been with the company for 20 years and there are only 160 people at their location. They met and the head of R&D found out the forklift driver had already optimized several ideas his team had been contemplating and that he had a few ideas R&D had never considered. Those ideas have now been incorporated into Char-Broil's line of smokers.

Two weeks later, another warehouse employee shared with Christine how he'd been assembling grills for 30 years and how he thought their instructions and processes could be much better. He even had a handwritten piece of paper taped to the wall near his workstation with a running list of his ideas.

That list has now been converted to an electronic document and this employee meets quarterly with the company's engineers to review his latest and best ideas for improvements and changes. All of this began by Christine letting people know it was okay to Speak Up, a very different operating norm for the company and then sharing these kinds of stories at all-employee meetings.

A Passion for Curiosity

Another reason people miss the obvious is when they are so familiar with a subject that they:

- Have forgotten what it's like not to have their vast knowledge, expertise and experience

- Feel a need to demonstrate their mastery of the subject to others

This is commonly referred to as the curse of knowledge, a concept more fully discussed in the book *Made To Stick: Why Some Ideas Survive and Others Die* by Dan and Chip Heath.

The curse of knowledge makes it harder for you to identify with another person's situation and explain things, such as a corporate strategy, in a manner that is easily understandable to someone who doesn't have your familiarity with the subject. The curse of knowledge also makes it harder for you to see things in new and novel ways.

There was a trait common among the leaders I interviewed that seems to have allowed them to overcome the curse of knowledge: **A passion for curiosity.**

They aren't afraid to ask what seem like obvious or stupid questions. And lots of them. These leaders know they will not be judged by the answers they give or their functional expertise, but by the quality of the questions they ask. They strive to enhance their understanding, knowledge and thinking continuously.

Adriano Pedrelli offers a great example of this trait. As CEO of WasteDry, an environmental services company that delivers eco-friendly solutions to the sewage issues of municipalities, communities and livestock farms, he has been among the first to challenge the status quo.

Adriano came into the company with much less understanding of the industry and the technology involved than the people working there. This lack of familiarity made it easier for Adriano to ask the stupid questions that got down to the reality of the problems being faced. He hasn't been hindered by the details of the years of research, patents and processes that came before him and could forge a profitable path to commercialization that, up until his arrival, had been missing in the company.

Some of the observations from our CEOs on seeing innovation and novelty were:

- **Give people the time, resources and permission they need to connect with people up, down, across the organization and outside of it.**

- **Create processes and opportunities that encourage people anywhere in the organization, at any level, to contribute their ideas and get credit for them**. Don't forget to ask your customers, both current and lost, lost prospects and vendors for their ideas.

- **Provide guardrails**. Constraints spark innovative thinking and boundaries help prevent feelings of being overwhelmed and frustrated by the possibilities.

- **Have a sincere interest in hearing what people have to say**, **regardless of their level.** The best way to demonstrate your sincerity is to implement some of their ideas.

- **Lead by example**. Just as the speed of the leader drives the speed of the team, **developing a more innovative culture starts at the top and is amplified by middle managers.** This applies to your openness to new ideas, how you react to failures and nearly everything you do.

- **Leading by example also applies to the organization's tolerance for risk and how it reacts to failures**. Again, guardrails and boundaries are helpful here. At the same time, try to be like Thomas Edison. When he was looking for the best filament for the electric light bulb: He didn't fail. He simply found 10,000 ways that didn't work.

- **Be an advocate of fast prototyping.** Ugly, shared and working now is a much better formula than perfect, secret, and useless later. Todd Brook, CEO of EnvisionIt, expressed it this way: *"Make it up, make it happen, make it reoccur."*

Brad Rex is an excellent example of what can happen when you bring all of this together.

Brad went from leading all aspects of Epcot Center for Walt Disney World Company to being President and CEO of Foundation Partners Group, a roll-up of what is now 90 funeral homes in 17 states. His mission was to grow Foundation Partners' business, in part, by changing the end-of-life planning experience. And who should know more about customer experiences than Disney? But Brad didn't come in and start dictating changes. He took the time to understand the market, the industry and to learn what was working and not working by asking customers, funeral directors and many others what they thought.

Among the first opportunities he identified was eliminating the traditional process for selecting a casket / urn: *"Designed to lower the anxiety of the Family and to increase the ability to plan a meaningful remembrance event. No Family has to walk into the discomfort of a cold, uncomfortable casket or urn selection room. This (redesigned) room setting gives the Family a warm living room environment. Using technology and a large screen format, Families are able to participate in the arrangement conversation with access to all options and total transparency on products, services and cost."*[4]

Other changes Brad and his team have since introduced include funeral webcasting, themed remembrance events and destination locations for services. While Brad has left Foundation Partners since being interviewed, his vision helped to reinvent the funeral experience and industry by bringing new ideas and innovation to an industry that many would describe as mature, fragmented, low single digit growth rate and offering well-established products and services.

Getting buy-in and support for implementing these changes and the results they led to would not have been possible without Brad carefully listening to what others thought.

Three Exercises to **Build Your Courage Muscles**

➢ **Ask yourself these two questions to see if you may be too comfortable with the status quo:**

    – How many of your discussions about new opportunities end in no decision?

    – How many of your projects and opportunities are stalled or stuck?

➢ **Your customers look to you to keep them from becoming complacent.** Assemble a group of them, including a few of your "not so good" customers. Ask them what you could be doing to improve the value you add to their businesses. One of the benefits will be how they'll resell themselves on your brand without you having to do anything.

➢ **At the next meeting of your direct reports, add to the agenda a discussion of the risks of staying on the course you're on.**

Take Aways to **Be Leading With Courage**

➤ Complacency is the biggest threat facing your business.

➤ The status quo may be comfortable, safe, and the "devil you know," but it's your biggest rival and a persistent Covert Change Killer.

➤ Leading With Courage usually requires you to be among the first to challenge the status quo.

➤ Challenging the status quo involves change, which nobody likes because it represents risk, frequently involves conflict, and usually requires a reallocation of time and resources – in the near term.

➤ The alternative to accepting the status quo is a business that will become irrelevant. The slide to the ultimate destination may take generations but stops along the way are likely to include hand wringing, second-guessing, cost cutting, commoditization and loss of respect.

Notes

Notes

Chapter 10

Craft A Winning Strategy

"Strategy without tactics is the slowest route to victory.
Tactics without strategy is the noise before defeat."
Sun Tzu

When a new leader or manager is appointed, it's common for them to come in with mandates to accelerate growth and improve profitability. These directives are usually accompanied by pressure to make an impact quickly. And let's not forget the need to attract and retain quality talent.

Come to think of it, it seems like we're talking about a set of strategic issues that are common to all organizations, doesn't it?

Well, looks can be deceiving.

Though organizations can have similar needs, there are plenty of differences upon a closer look. The circumstances are unique. Cultures can vary greatly. Before long, it becomes quite apparent that the perfect solution for one company is unlikely to deliver the same result at another.

Here are just a few of the issues the CEOs I spoke to said they have encountered:

- The Board of Directors was growing impatient with how long it was taking for the current, well-researched strategy to show results.

- A major competitor had launched a well-publicized change in its strategy

- A firm's services were rapidly becoming commodities

- There had been a significant shift in technology that rendered a company's products obsolete

- New regulations were being enacted that required some key products to be reformulated, relabeled, registered, recalled, etc.

- The company's industry was consolidating

- The firm just lost a long-term, major client that they thought liked their services.

- One of their colleagues was at the center of a highly-publicized harassment scandal.

- They hadn't been developing their next generation of leaders

Each of these circumstances and situations called for unique solutions and tactics. The CEOs tackled these problems by developing strategic, operating and marketing plans that were tailor-made for their companies. Without exception, applying a cookie-cutter wasn't an option.

This brings us to another blind spot to avoid in order to effectively be leading with courage: **Failing to develop and implement a winning strategy that fulfills the mandates you've been given within the timeframe granted.**

True, this is no small challenge. If it were a simple and obvious task, the search I conducted on "*corporate strategy*" on Amazon.com wouldn't have identified 42,355 available titles on the subject!

So where do you begin in your process for developing such plans? Let's rely on the wisdom from some of the leaders who have contributed to this book. In their eyes, well-crafted plans incorporate:

- **How you will create value** by solving other peoples' problems

- **How you will deliver value** in the form of capabilities and resources

- **How you will capture / profit from the value you create and deliver** – monetizing your efforts

- Awareness that your business model will not last and **how you plan to remain relevant** in an ever-changing environment

Christine Robins, CEO of Char-Broil LLC, told me how she didn't come into her role with the answer. She knew it was essential to come up with a winning strategy quickly and that it would better to get it 85% right to get people settled down, focused on what the future looks like and knowing how they can make an impact. Tweaks, fine tuning and other adjustments could be rendered once the strategy was rolled out and broader input was sought. She knew it was going to be more about the employees executing a plan and less about her as a leader and her management team.

Christine worked with her management team to understand the current strategy of the company, its history and culture and where they were today. She wanted them to build on their strengths and weaknesses as an organization so as not to be like someone else.

For example, when Christine arrived at Char-Broil, she said she probably heard the name of their biggest competitor ten times a day. Now, that company's name is never mentioned. Christine told me how *"we own our destiny, we own who we're going to be, and we're going to win the way we want to win."* Under Chris' leadership, Char-Broil has gone from growing 2%-3% per year to double-digit growth and she's confident they will be able to do this for the next five years.

Even Smart People Can Plan Poorly…

When intelligent businesspeople are missing some of these essential elements of proper strategic planning, bad things happen that are difficult to recover from.

Three such historical examples come to mind in the business world – by the way, all organizations run by some brilliant individuals, too:

- **RCA Expands Much Too Far** In the 1960s, RCA began to diversify beyond the scope of its traditional business. It bought publisher Random House in 1965, car rental company Hertz in 1967 and frozen food maker Banquet in 1970. The company was eventually sold to General Electric Co. in 1986.

• **Time Warner and AOL's Marriage That Never Should Have Been** In February 2000, Time Warner and AOL merged. Shortly afterward, the growth and profitability of AOL slowed to a crawl due in part to the burst of the "dot com bubble" and the economic recession that followed the attack on the Twin Towers on September 11, 2001. The market capitalization of AOL Time Warner plummeted from $226 billion...to $20 billion.

Journalist Tim Arango, in a New York Times article on the subject, wrote:

> *"To call (the Time Warner-AOL transaction) the worst in history...does not begin to tell the story of how some of the brightest minds in technology and media collaborated to produce a deal now regarded by many as a colossal mistake."*

• **Kodak Ignores The Digital Camera** Kodak invented digital photography in 1975, but the proliferation of the digital camera undid its fortunes by companies like Canon and Nikon that ended up dominating the market.

Steve Sasson, the Kodak engineer who invented the first digital camera, characterized the initial corporate response to his invention this way: *"It was filmless photography, so management's reaction was, 'That's cute – but don't tell anyone about it.'"*

This excerpt from a 2011 New York Times article sums it up quite well:

> *"Kodak management not only presided over the creation of this technological break-through, but was also presented with an accurate market assessment about the risks and opportunities of such capabilities. Yet, Kodak failed in making the right strategic choices."*

Nobody wants to go down in history as the next significant case study in poor planning that could've been avoided, so here's a short list intended to remind you of the characteristics of plans that work.

The best plans are:

- **Well researched** - Plans that will make an impact are based on market facts and realities, not on the perceptions of what an organization's leaders think their customers want and need.

- **Written down** - Having a tangible artifact of the effort and thinking that went into preparing it ensures that the plan is clear and communicated consistently.

- **Crystal clear** - Good plans are specific on what is to be achieved – and how. They avoid jargon. The measures of success are dates and numbers that can be graphed. The measures are also SMART (Specific, Measurable, Achievable, Results-focused and Time constrained).

- **Based on your strengths** - Good plans leverage your organization's strengths relative to your competition. These are the attributes and characteristics that *truly* differentiate you from the rest of the pack.
The fact that you've got really smart people, put your customers' interests first, and act with integrity may sound good, but you need to take those off your list now. Why? While they may be part of how you describe your organization, they do not make you different from others.

- **Eliminate distractions** - Plans that make an impact focus the entire organization on a few, most important things. They provide the utmost clarity on what should and should not be done.
As a leader, this is one of your most important roles. Todd Brook, Founder of Envisionit, captured this well. He reminded me how the word "decide" is derived from the same root as suicide, homicide, pesticide, and herbicide – it means to kill off. Deciding is often thought of as the selection of a path, when, as Todd pointed out, it really means proactively taking options off the table.

- **Reviewed on a regular basis** - When plans are reviewed periodically, they become living documents that need to be updated to reflect meaningful changes in your environment. If you want to change your plan because it's not delivering the results you expected, make sure you've been faithful to executing the strategies you chose. Poor results tend to be driven by poor implementation, commitment and follow-through.

Let's face it – developing and implementing a successful plan doesn't happen overnight. As you drive your strategy forward, communicate a deep and genuine respect for what the organization has accomplished up to this point. Consider the impact first (including its unintended consequences), then the change you want to drive. Let the sources of organization pride determine your priorities and pace.

Jude Rake, a two-time CEO who also held leadership positions at Clorox, PepsiCo, Kodak and SC Johnson & Son, emphasized a key point – it's less about the plan and more about the planning. Looking back over all the strategic plans he worked on, Jude admitted many of them were mediocre at best. But he said they won because *"...we were all working together on it, we planned it together, we had skin in the game, we had ownership and our engagement went up."*

Jude has found that it takes about six months to build engagement around the plan. In those instances where his clients have told him it can be done faster than that, it seems to take them more time. The CEO of one of his clients described the changes initiated by Jude's planning process this way: *"This place is totally different. We've got people running all over the place with new ideas. They're excited about the business. And the reason they're so excited is no one ever asked (them to participate).*

Accomplish More by Setting 75-Day Objectives And Deliverables

When I interviewed Hardik Bhatt in 2017, he was the Chief Information Officer for the State of Illinois. Now, he leads the Digital Government initiative for Amazon Web Services, is an angel investor, and serves on the Board of Directors of Fermi National Labs. Hardik shared with me how he likes to break everything down into 75-day objectives and deliverables.

Why 75 days? Hardik told his leadership team they would be taking a page out of the playbook of the President of the United States. He or she gets elected on the second Tuesday of November and takes office on January 20th, which is anywhere between 74 and 77 days, depending on the calendar year. Hardik said *"If the president is ready to run the country in 75 days, we should be able to at least hit a milestone in the same amount of time. Let's break everything down."*

This was a departure from more traditional time frames of 90 days, 100 days or longer. There were going to four cycles each year, with each cycle having a different start and end date versus a quarterly end date. This kept everybody on the edge and understanding what they needed to deliver. Hardik then started holding each of his leaders accountable for developing 75-day plans and deliverables.

What's nice about this project management hack is how it gives a leader or manager a long list of quick wins to talk about. Hardik remembers people noticing how *"There's a lot of activity going on here and a lot of results."* This was opposed to waiting for that first cycle, which was usually a year.

Shorter time frames also made it easier for Hardik to talk about what his team would accomplish in very concrete ways. For example, if it was a procurement initiative, when are we going to finish writing the scope of work? When are we going to finish publishing the procurement spec? When are we going to finish getting evaluations done? When are we going to finish the contract?

By the way, this technique doesn't just apply to large, complex tasks. Hardik's first 75 days had simple things like, *"Go and meet with as many internal people as possible."* He remembered how he completely cut himself off for the first 75 days from the outside world and just focused on understanding the inside.

Three Exercises to **Build Your Courage Muscles**

➢ **Answer these questions about the five most recent plans you've prepared and executed:**

- How many of these plans have delivered the results they promised?

- What did you do particularly well in developing, communicating and executing the most successful plans?

- What did you fail to do well when you were disappointed by the results of these plans?

➢ **Gather together three or four of your direct reports and prepare a SWOT analysis (Strengths, Weaknesses, Opportunities, Threats) that is based on how you compare to your competitors**. Challenge each other to be brutally honest in your assessments. Done correctly, you'll have identified more Weaknesses than Strengths and Opportunities.

➢ **At the beginning of your next objective-setting cycle, tell your direct reports how you will be holding them accountable for the commitments the two of you have agreed to.** Explain to each of them what the consequences will be and the follow-through on your promise. To be fair, when they exceed your expectations, there should be a clearly defined reward for doing so. Put all of this in writing to avoid ambiguity, poor memories and a lack of resolve on everyone's part.

Take Aways to **Be Leading With Courage**

➤ Your ability to craft and implement plans will be among your legacies as a leader

➤ The biggest threat to your plans is the lack of commitment to following through on them – both yours and the people entrusted to execute them.

➤ Holding people accountable for their commitments to the best of their abilities without any reminders is essential.

➤ Your people also have to know there are consequences for not meeting their commitments. When they don't, you cannot waiver in demonstrating you were serious about it. No excuses. No rationalizations. No "next time." Because someone will test your resolve, a lot of eyes will be watching how you react, and everyone's behavior going forward will be based on what you do.

Notes

(Chapter 11

Bringing It All Together

"Courage is what it takes to stand up and speak;
courage is also what it takes to sit down and listen."
Winston Churchill

Armed with the insights and perspectives of the CEOs I interviewed for this book, I have attempted to simplify a complex problem: ***What are the essential behaviors of Leading With Courage?***

30 interviews and nearly 50 hours of audio recordings later, I've identified **26 attributes**, that collectively define Leading With Courage.

How do you efficiently comprehend all 26 traits of leadership? Not to worry. I've divided the 26 attributes into four broader categories. Each of those categories has six or seven attributes and none of those attributes have been assigned to multiple categories.

The four categories of Leading With Courage are:

➤ **Astute Generalist**

➤ **All-Star Relationship Builder**

➤ **Champion of the Culture and Sustainable Competitive Advantage**

➤ **Courageous Decision Maker**

Below is the assignment of the attributes to these categories, which should explain what is meant by each of them:

Astute Generalist

> - Functional expertise alone is a liability
> - Understands the organization's parts and pieces
> - Fluent on how the business makes money, differentiates and grows
> - Understands how his or her industry / profession works
> - Lifelong learner
> - Passion for curiosity

All-Star Relationship Builder

> - Skilled at building relationships and networking
> - Genuinely cares about and is interested in others
> - Regularly solicits feedback and perspectives from wide range of stakeholders
> - Good listener
> - Transparent communicator
> - Creates alignment that fosters trust

Champion of the Culture and Sustainable Competitive Advantage

> - Role model for honoring the business' culture
> - Thinks strategically
> - Guided by optimizing the long-term value of the business
> - Among the first to challenge the status quo
> - Spots trends and threats
> - Focuses on fewer, bigger opportunities
> - Delivers crisp and compelling messages

Courageous Decision Maker

> - Inclusive problem solver
> - Balances gut with analytics
> - Keeps an open-mind
> - Before making a decision, considers the unintended consequences

➢ Not afraid of disappointing those whose views don't prevail
➢ Draws a line in the sand and sticks with it
➢ Holds people accountable for their commitments

What's also interesting about the list is how each of the attributes is related to the successful execution of strategic and operating plans. This makes a lot of sense when you consider that the ability to deliver results is how leaders are judged and it's the mandate they are given when they move into their positions. So, the list provides insights into the obstacles that must be overcome for a leader or manager to be successful.

Take Our Leading With Courage Self-Assessment – The Final Exercise To Build Your Courage Muscles

Shortly after grouping the 26 attributes into four categories, I was also struck by how the model lends itself to an online self-assessment. So, I've created just that. Upon completing this self-assessment, you'll immediately receive your overall score and a rating.

Those ratings are:

➢ **Effective Leader With Courage**

➢ **Brave Leader**

➢ **Emerging Leader**

➢ **Aspiring Leader**

The overall rating is then followed by a one-page report that shows 1) how you scored yourself on each attribute, 2) a score for each category and 3) the overall score. We've also created a second report that shows you based on your scoring of the 26 attributes, which of the nine blind spots or behaviors of Leading With Courage you **may** need to be on the alert for.

I emphasize the word "may" because this second report is not predictive of which behaviors you will need to avoid or recover from. But based on the nearly 3,000 people who have filled it out, we've learned the following:

➢ The more experience you have, the fewer behaviors that are flagged

➢ The average person has 2.75 blind spots identified by the assessment

➢ The three most common blind spots are attempting to do much yourself (i.e., need help with delegation), sticking with under-performers too long (i.e., having some challenges building a high-performing team, and focusing on fewer and bigger ideas / projects (this is part delegation skills and part challenges with prioritization).

The other "caveat" of the tool is it is a self-assessment and prone to positive bias. Like all self-assessments, the results are based on only your view, which are usually suspect. For this reason we prefer 180- and 360-assessments when identifying and understanding our blind spots, but self-assessments are a good place to start.

To take our leadership self-assessment, type the URL below into your browser and you'll be taken to it:

http://bit.ly/gotosa

The Most Critical and Difficult of the Four Categories

Nearly every executive interviewed for this book believes that being a **Courageous Decision Maker** is the most challenging of the four categories. This is because the other categories have attributes that can be learned, improved upon with practice and even compensated for with mastery of some of the others. But a leader must own courageous decision-making, with its "buck stops here" mentality. Its quality and timeliness will likely define his or her tenure in the role.

Another factor that seems to make this the most difficult of the four categories is how most of want to be liked and there are aspects of this category that could run contrary to this. For example, being able to a draw a line in the stand once a decision is made and not being afraid to disappoint people whose views aren't being supported may not always win you friends. But these are examples of some of the tough things leaders have to do. Others include:

> ➤ Modeling the expected behaviors
> ➤ Messaging expectations
> ➤ Managing situations
> ➤ Monitoring the workplace

This statistic from a *McKinsey Quarterly* survey published in January 2009 shows just how tough it is to make good decisions:

> *"Of 2,207 executives, only 28% said that the quality of strategic decisions in their companies was generally good. 60% thought that bad decisions were about as frequent as good ones. The remaining 12% thought good decisions were altogether infrequent."*

Safe Decisions Aren't Safe

In early 2016, Mike Myatt, an author and columnist focused on leadership, shared in Forbes Magazine his list of the five decisions many people consider as "being safe." Leaders and managers who are Leading With Courage regard these decisions as anything but safe.

Mike's list appears below, along with a few modifications based on the insights from the leaders I interviewed for this book:

1. The Politically Correct Decision:

Those who are Leading With Courage don't seek to be politically correct – they seek to *be correct.* They find being politically correct rarely solves problems and often makes them worse.

The first step in solving problems and making real change is to deal in whole truths, not hidden agendas, untruths or partial truths.

2. The Hiring Decision:

Leaders and managers who are committed to Leading With Courage don't hire the best available person – they hire *the best person.* Period.

They don't compromise by settling for what's expedient or safe. Compromise has its place in negotiations, but it has no role in talent acquisition and management. When leaders make a bad hiring or promotion decision, they have no one to blame but themselves.

One of our consulting clients had the practice of having candidates for senior positions meet with a psychologist before finalizing their offers. Based on his interview and deep understanding of the organization's culture, the psychologist would make a *"hire / do not hire"* recommendation. But when our client started to have some serious issues fitting several people into key positions, we looked deeper into the psychologist's reports. We were surprised to learn that, without exception, the recommendations were "do not hire."

When the leader of the organization was asked if he was aware of this, he said that didn't surprise him. He then explained how the company overrode the psychologist's recommendations because the positions had been open for such an extended period of time. Therefore, they felt they could "rehab" the person and the person could adapt to their culture.

We then asked the leader why he continued to send people to interview with a psychologist if he was going to override the recommendation. After all, why not save the time and expense incurred by all parties? He had no answer for this.

3. The Values Decision:

Rewarding performance over values might seem to be safe or smart, but it is neither. Organizations have core values for a reason – to give them a true north. Organizational values exist to align interests, actions and direction. Ultimately, values exist to create a high-trust environment where exceptional performance is the rule and not the exception.

When leaders and managers make decisions that contradict core values, there is a steep price to pay – a loss of trust. When a leader talks about values but fails to act on or defend them, the entire enterprise is placed at risk.

A characteristic of Leading With Courage is **zero tolerance** for actions and/or decisions that constitute a violation of the organization's culture or values.

We regularly find this type of decision to be a challenge for leaders of professional services firms when one of their "rainmakers" is behaving badly. If that rainmaker is also perceived as being loved by his or her clients, which tends to be the case, it seems that he or she can get away with practically anything as long as the act is chargeable to a client.

The leaders of these organizations are fully aware of the dysfunction this creates among other partners and staff. Yet, many tolerate it for some good, but mostly bad reasons, such as:

➤ Addressing the problem will create conflict (and the person using this excuse is conflict-averse)

➤ It involves a senior partner

➤ The partner is a famous person in the industry

➤ The person is a few years away from retirement

➤ They've been a good partner until now

➤ *"Our clients won't understand."*

4. The Managed Decision:

Many leaders believe if they can manage enough aspects of a decision, it will be safe to make. But when decisions are over-managed, they tend to be ineffective.

Author and columnist Mike Myatt is fond of saying, *"managing expectations is gamesmanship – aligning them is leadership."*

Those who are Leading With Courage provide a compass, but they don't draw the map. Thinking in terms of guidelines and guardrails – rather than regulations and rules – effectively Leading With Courage means you are building the right team and have the confidence to allow decisions to be made closest to the front lines.

5. The No Decision:

The reality is, not making a decision is still a decision – it's usually just not the *right* decision.

Avoiding a decision doesn't mean you'll avoid the issue, but that you'll have fewer options for addressing it. And waiting to make a decision or avoiding a decision may well be what got you into the problem you're facing. Those who are Leading With Courage don't find safety by sticking their heads in the sand. Instead, they find safety in consistently tackling issues and making good decisions.

Adding to this challenge is how it is lonely at the top. Diane Strong, the owner and president of the staffing agency Manpower of West Virginia, relayed a story that captured this so well.

When Diane was a little girl, she was riding a horse that suddenly took off. Although she didn't know anything about horses, Diane was determined to hang onto that runaway horse. Fortunately, her Uncle was there and in a very authoritative voice told her to "Jump!" several times. Despite being scared, Diane leaped off the running horse and avoided being ripped apart by the barbed wire fence towards which the horse was galloping.

For the rest of the story to make sense, Diane told me how I needed to know that her husband, who was her business partner, coach and most-trusted advisor had passed away some years ago. This has left her as the leader of their 11-office staffing business that covers the state of West Virginia.

Diane shared with me how her biggest problem today is how she doesn't really have anyone to say, "Jump!" For example, when is it time to get bigger, buy more markets, open a new office, buy an existing business, start a new business or take up a hobby and relax?

It would be easy for Diane to become paralyzed and make no decisions, but she's driven and engaged in her business. Diane's persistence and resilience have allowed her to make tough strategic decisions, with the support of a great team, that have let her guide and take control of her destiny.

It's A Never-Ending Process

Being a leader or manager is as rewarding as it is tenuous. Your personal stock value rises and falls quickly and you're only as good as your last decision and the results it delivered.

A leader or manager's personal stock value can decline when:

He or she wants to be liked by everyone, is afraid to commit to an action plan or fails to take responsibility for his or her decisions.

Leaders and managers are expected to make choices. Even when done the "right way" it's likely not everyone will agree with them and you'll have to be comfortable making choices that some will find disappointing. Saying "yes" to everyone and everything is not the answer.

Think about it, if you say "yes" to everyone and your resources are limited, aren't you, in essence, saying "no" to someone?

Wouldn't it be more authentic and consistent with honoring your commitments and word to say "no" up-front, along with the rationale behind your choice? Wouldn't you prefer to be seen by others as credible, direct, and worthy of their trust?

As David Smith, a veteran CEO of publicly traded and privately held companies told me when I interviewed him, *"when there's a problem, do you tend to look out the window or in the mirror?"*

> ➤ **They become paralyzed by a fear of being criticized for the approach they take, get too comfortable with being comfortable or fail to take into consideration the unintended consequences of their plans before making a decision.**

> ➤ **They react badly when their feelings are hurt or fail to see or act on the threats or opportunities that are in front of them.** Or they are unable to rally their teams, whether that's around an objective or a change in direction.

How To Know When All Of This Is Having An Impact? Measure Employee Engagement.

At Leading With Courage Academy, we encourage clients to measure and track employee engagement to answer questions like "Is this leadership development program having any impact?" and "Are your efforts making a difference?" We go so far as to include a tool for measuring, visualizing, and improving employee engagement on a quarterly basis as an option in each of our assignments.

When assessed every 90 days, the causes for a lack of employee engagement cease to be blind spots and the measure becomes a leading indicator of employee and customer turnover and top- and bottom-line results.

We also encourage clients to use employee engagement to track the progress of integrating two cultures into one higher-performing organization following a buy-side merger or acquisition transaction. The time to think about the people affected by a deal is when you first start to talk about a merger or acquisition as a strategic option. Divide the employees into two groups – the acquiring company and the acquired company – and measure their respective levels of engagement on a regular basis. Don't be alarmed that if immediately after the transaction closes you see a gap between the groups. That will close when you're doing an excellent job of integrating the two organizations. Your goal should be for both groups to reach an even higher level of engagement than either had achieved prior to the transaction. How about that for synergy?

In all cases, employee engagement is a more reliable indicator of how things are going than relying solely on one's gut feel.

Stefan Wissenbach, founder of Engagement Multiplier, wrote in his 2016 book *The Engaged Organization* as follows:

> *When you're engaged, your relationships are stronger, your happiness levels rise, you accomplish more, and you have the power to achieve your most difficult goals.*
>
> *Engaged organizations are easier to run – they make more money, suffer less waste, and are happier places to work.*

Wissenbach, goes on to write:

> *The evidence is overwhelming, and yet many business owners still resist engagement. Or they dabble (dangerously) in it and then (unfortunately) abandon it, because they haven't quite managed to separate the myths surrounding engagement from the reality. If these reluctant business owners knew the statistics and understood how to set up a foolproof engagement framework, they would change their minds.*

So, here are a few statistics that will help you understand why employee engagement, which is the ability for employees to be present, focused, and energized at work, should be one of the few indicators of the health of your business that you should be following.

- ➢ **70%** of the variance in employee engagement scores can be attributed to Managers. (Gallup)

- ➢ Of employees who rate their boss unfavorable, **40%** interviewed for a new job in the past three months versus **10%** who rated their manager highly favorable. (TINYpulse)

- ➢ More than **80%** of workers are either actively looking for a new job or are open to one (Ajilon)

> Organizations with high employee engagement outperform those with low employee engagement by **202%**. (Business2Community)

> **88%** of employers think employees leave for money; meanwhile only **12%** actually leave for money. (Gallup)

> Companies with engaged employees see **233%** greater customer loyalty. (Aberdeen Group)

> Organizations with the most engaged employees achieve **65%** greater share-price increase, **15%** greater employee productivity, and **20%** less absenteeism. (Queens School of Business)

We believe that employee engagement can be a source of competitive advantage. It's a differentiator when it's considered a highly-contagious virus that affects everyone who comes into contact with an Engaged Organization including its suppliers, consultants, customers, families of its employees, and members of the communities the organization serves. To demonstrate our commitment to creating Engaged Organizations, the Leading With Courage Academy is an authorized partner of Engagement Multiplier which allows us to help businesses move from blind spots to action to higher-performing organizations.

Each of the blind spots identified and discussed in this book has the potential to be career limiting. When they are avoided, minimized or nimbly recovered from, the odds of being among the 40% of leaders who fail, quit or are pushed out during their first 18 months in the job are much less. Still, you can never rest on your laurels.

The process begins again each time:

> Your company is acquired or brings in private equity investors
> You get a new boss
> The next generation of a family-owned enterprise enters the business
> You expand into a new country or begin serving a new segment of the market
> There's a major change in leadership at one of your key customers or clients

> ➤ You find it necessary to replace one of your trusted resources or advisors

By Leading With Courage, you are better-equipped to handle these changes. They have the courage and wisdom to do the right thing, which (ret) Major General John Borling defined this way:

> ➤ *The courage to transform myself into something new rather than to walk away in retreat*
> ➤ *The courage to say "this is not right and I'm going to do something else," even when it's at your economic disadvantage*
> ➤ *It is the courage to say "I'm wrong"*
> ➤ *It is the courage to say "I'm sorry"*
> ➤ *It is the courage to say "I don't know"*
> ➤ *It is the courage to ask the group whom you have been entrusted to lead "help me find a new direction" without fear of losing your authority or position*

If you are one of these special leaders or managers, you will see changes as opportunities rather than risks and you will proactively manage them. You will maintain a positive attitude that's visible to others and will be confident in your ability to remain humble. All the while, you will demonstrate why you are the right person for the job.

A Final Three Take Aways to **Be Leading With Courage**

- ➤ Authority, position and title do not equal leadership

    - Leadership is about what you do, not where you're seated
    - Authority can compel others to take action, but it does little to inspire belief

- ➤ Leadership is about relationships and influence

    - Leadership happens when your influence causes people to work towards a shared vision
    - Influence and significance come from caring about and growing others
    - Leadership is about inspiring and motivating ourselves and others to create high-performing teams and engaged organizations

- ➤ Being self-aware is a never-ending journey

    - Have the courage to seek feedback
    - Self-awareness keeps you relevant

My wish for you is that this book will help bring you peace of mind and confidence from:

> ➢ Creating your leadership role, not just filling it.
> ➢ Seizing your leadership moments when they present themselves.
> ➢ Making an impact – faster and bigger than expected.
> ➢ Motivating and retaining the people you are leading.

Remember: Everyone deserves to work for a high-performing, engaged organization. And the people you lead expect the "best you" you can give.

Notes

Lee H. Eisenstaedt, MBA
Founder, Leading With Courage® Academy, LLC

Lee Eisenstaedt brings more than 35 years of diverse finance and operations experience to the clients of the Leading With Courage® Academy ("LWCA").

The CFO of a multi-billion dollar, multi-national company described Lee as a well-rounded executive because he had *"...worked in more than two functions, for more than two companies, in more than two countries."* In late 2015, a leader with a national association of attorneys serving family-held businesses described him as a *"Renaissance Man of Business."*

At LWCA, Lee helps teams and individuals more clearly understand themselves and how others see them, with greater peace of mind and confidence that comes from being more effective leaders, being the outcome. This is done by designing and facilitating *measurable* leadership development workshops, assessments, and coaching programs that move clients from identifying their blind spots to action so they can motivate and retain their employees and build more engaged, higher-performing organizations.

Prior to LWCA, Lee was a founding partner of L. Harris Partners, LLC, during which time he surveyed/ interviewed several thousand clients of professional services firms. He has been a Chief Operating Officer of a Top 5 and Top 50 CPA firm. Lee spent the majority of his career, 22 years, with the SC Johnson family of companies – including the consumer products company, the SC Johnson family office and Johnson Outdoors, Inc. – in the

U.S. and Western Europe, frequently as the "right hand" to the leader of the division, subsidiary or country to which he was assigned.

During his two European assignments, Lee lived and worked in Paris, France for five years and had responsibility for finance, accounting, logistics, IT and customer service in five countries within the European Union. In the U.S., Lee served as Senior Director, Corporate Services and Facilities, Controller of several divisions, a "global professor" of strategic planning, Director of Business Development and Venture Manager. Lee also spent six years with Baxter International, Inc. in various finance and accounting positions.

Lee is the co-author of the book "Wallet Share: Grow Your Practice Without Adding Clients," and is a frequent speaker at national and regional conferences on leadership and client loyalty. He is also a regular contributor to Forbes.com on leadership-related matters.

Lee received his MBA from Northwestern University and his B.A. from Franklin & Marshall College. He has attended executive programs on marketing at Harvard, Wharton and Northwestern Universities and weeklong executive development programs at INSEAD and the Center for Creative Leadership. Lee is also an Official Member of the Forbes Coaches Council, an authorized partner and trainer of Everything DiSC® and Five Behavior of a Cohesive trainer, a certified practitioner of Genos International's suite of emotional intelligence assessments, an authorized partner of Engagement Multiplier, and a Net Promoter® Certified Associate.

www.ingramcontent.com/pod-product-compliance
Lightning Source LLC
Chambersburg PA
CBHW071848200326
41519CB00016B/4294